FSC
www.fsc.org
MIX
Papier aus verantwortungsvollen Quellen
Paper from responsible sources
FSC® C105338

Steffen Blomberg

The realisation of offshore wind park projects in Germany

Political environment, legal framework and bankability implications

Anchor Academic
Publishing

Blomberg, Steffen: The realisation of offshore wind park projects in Germany - political environment, legal framework and bankability implications. Hamburg, Anchor Academic Publishing 2013

Buch-ISBN: 978-3-95489-092-7
PDF-eBook-ISBN: 978-3-95489-592-2
Druck/Herstellung: Anchor Academic Publishing, Hamburg, 2013

Bibliografische Information der Deutschen Nationalbibliothek:
Die Deutsche Nationalbibliothek verzeichnet diese Publikation in der Deutschen Nationalbibliografie; detaillierte bibliografische Daten sind im Internet über http://dnb.d-nb.de abrufbar.

Bibliographical Information of the German National Library:
The German National Library lists this publication in the German National Bibliography. Detailed bibliographic data can be found at: http://dnb.d-nb.de

Hermannstal 119k, 22119 Hamburg
http://www.diplomica-verlag.de, Hamburg 2013
Printed in Germany

Abstract

According to the German government's recently introduced new energy concept, renewable energies shall replace fossil and nuclear energy sources step-by-step. The offshore wind energy sector plays a key role in this new energy strategy and shall contribute the major share of renewable energy to the future German energy mix. The purpose of this work is to examine and evaluate the applicable conditions to be considered by project developers and investors when realising an offshore wind park project in Germany. Firstly, it analyses the political environment for the offshore wind energy sector in Germany. Secondly, it gives an overview of the most relevant German legal statutes determining, inter alia, the establishment of wind energy priority areas, the applicable German feed-in tariff scheme and the necessary approval process for offshore wind parks to be erected in the German exclusive economic zone. Thirdly, potential bankability issues and financing challenges are discussed which an offshore wind park project planner might be exposed to when trying to secure a debt financing for such a sophisticated and capital-intensive project. The result of the investigation is that offshore wind park project developers can rely on a very supporting political environment and a sustainable legal framework in Germany, which provide for the investment security and planning reliability urgently needed. Furthermore, financing challenges for German offshore wind park projects have been considerably reduced lately. Overall, the conditions for the realisation of offshore wind parks in Germany should be very encouraging for project developers and investors nowadays and constitute a solid and reliable basis for the targeted strong growth of the offshore wind energy sector in Germany in the near future.

Key Words: offshore wind park, German exclusive economic zone, renewable energies act, feed-in tariff, governmental measures, wind energy priority areas, approval process, bankability, financing challenges

Author's Email Address: steffenblomberg@web.de

Acknowledgements

I would like to express my gratitude to all those who have contributed to this work.

I'm grateful to Mr. Christian Dahlke, Head of Division Management of the Sea at the Federal Maritime and Hydrographic Agency, for being available to exchange views about the mandatory approval process for offshore wind parks to be erected in the German exclusive economic zone and for giving me an update on the recent (political) developments in this regard.

Furthermore, I would like to thank my colleagues working in the renewable energies department at KfW IPEX Bank GmbH, one of the leading players in offshore wind park (project) finance in Europe and the leading bank when it comes to the financing of offshore wind parks in Germany. Particular thanks go to Mr. Peter Schäfer, Mr. Mirko Sedlacek and Mr. Andrew Eckhardt for the advice provided and for giving me the opportunity to get a practical insight into this field and the financing challenges related to it.

Last but not least, I wish to express my sincere thanks to Dr. Oliver Lohse, who has drawn my interest to the field of renewable energies and the offshore wind energy sector in particular, with his energy finance class held at the Institute for Law and Finance at the Goethe-University Frankfurt am Main, Germany, for his helpful suggestions and valuable comments.

Table of Contents

List of Figures

List of Abbreviations

BEL	Belgium
bn	billion (*Milliarde*)
CEAR	Construction/Erection All Risks (insurance)
CMS	Condition Monitoring System
DEN	Denmark
DSCR	Debt Service Coverage Ratio
EEZ	Exclusive Economic Zone (*ausschließliche Wirtschaftszone*)
EI-Act (*EnWG*)	Energy Industry Act (*Energiewirtschaftsgesetz*)
EIA (*UVP*)	Environmental Impact Assessment (*Umweltverträglichkeitsprüfung*)
EIA-Act (*UVPG*)	Environmental Impact Assessment Act (*Umweltverträglichkeitsprüfungsgesetz*)
EIB	European Investment Bank
EKF	Eksport Kredit Fonden
EPCI	Engineering, Procurement, Construction and Installation (contract)
EST	Estonia
EU	European Union
EUR	Euro
EURIBOR	Euro InterBank Offered Rate
EWEA	European Wind Energy Association
FANC (*BfN*)	Federal Agency for Nature Conservation (*Bundesamt für Naturschutz*)
FEA (*UBA*)	Federal Environment Agency (*Umweltbundesamt*)
FEM (*BUM*)	Federal Environment Ministry (*Bundesumweltministerium*)
FMHA (*BSH*)	Federal Maritime and Hydrographic Agency (*Bundesamt für Seeschifffahrt und Hydrographie*)
FMRA (*SeeAufgG*)	Federal Maritime Responsibilities Act (*Seeaufgabengesetz*)
FNCA (*BNatSchG*)	Federal Nature Conservation Act (*Bundesnaturschutzgesetz*)
FSPA (*ROG*)	Federal Spatial Planning Act (*Raumordnungsgesetz*)
GCC *(BGB)*	German Civil Code *(Bürgerliches Gesetzbuch)*

GEAA (*NABEG*)	Grid Expansion Acceleration Act (*Gesetz über Maßnahmen zur Beschleunigung des Netzausbaus Elektrizitätsnetze*)
GER	Germany
GFNA (*BNetzA*)	German Federal Network Agency (*Bundesnetzagentur*)
IPAA (*InfraStrPlanVBeschlG*)	Infrastructure Planning Acceleration Act (*Infrastrukturplanungsbeschleunigungsgesetz*)
IRL	Ireland
KfW	Kreditanstalt für Wiederaufbau
KfW IPEX	KfW IPEX Bank GmbH
km	kilometer(s)
kwh	kilowatt-hour(s)
m	meter(s)
m/s	meter(s) per second
MFO (*SeeAnlV*)	Marine Facilities Ordinance (*Seeanlagenverordnung*)
mn	million (*Million*)
MW	megawatt
NED	Netherlands
O&M	Operation & Maintenance
OWG	Offshore Wind Generator(s) (*Offshore-Windanlage(n)*)
OWP	Offshore Wind Park(s)
RE-Act (*EEG*)	Renewable Energies Act (*Erneuerbare-Energien-Gesetz*)
SPC	Single Purpose Company (*Einzweckgesellschaft*)
STEA (*StUK*)	Standards for the Environmental Impact Assessment (*Standarduntersuchungskonzept*)
SWE	Sweden
TSO	Transmission System Operator(s) (*Übertragungsnetzbetreiber*)
UK	United Kingdom
UNCLOS (*SRÜ*)	United Nations Convention on the Law of the Sea (*Seerechtsübereinkommen der Vereinten Nationen*)
WSD	Waterways and Shipping Directorate (*Wasser- und Schifffahrtsdirektion*)

1. Introduction

1.1 Motivation and objective

According to the German government the future German energy mix shall be mainly based on renewable energy sources. Offshore wind energy plays a key role in this new energy strategy and is expected to provide the major share of renewable energy to be produced in Germany in the future. Nevertheless, the German offshore wind energy sector has developed much slower than expected, despite considerable supporting efforts taken by the government. Compared to other European countries, there is only little installed offshore wind energy capacity available in Germany today, but the German legislator's medium-term growth targets for this industry are enormous.

In this context, the following two questions are to be asked: Does the German government turn a blind eye to the contradictory development just mentioned and/or is there reason for hope that the German offshore wind energy sector will accelerate and grow much stronger in the future?

The purpose of this work is to describe the general conditions applicable in Germany, which a project developer or potential investor has to consider when planning an offshore wind park (OWP) in the German exclusive economic zone (EEZ).[1] Furthermore, it analyses specific challenges related to the realisation of such kind of projects, identifies existing problems, and outlines possible solutions where appropriate. In doing so, the following chapters will mainly focus on the political environment for the offshore wind energy industry in Germany, the relevant legal framework applicable when realising an OWP, as well as on the bankability challenges a project developer might be exposed to when trying to secure a debt financing for an OWP project in Germany.

Apart from giving a theoretical overview about the main subjects referred to above, this work also tries to address recent developments one can observe in practice. Hence, personal interviews have been conducted with experienced practitioners to get

[1] Despite the fact that this work is mainly written through the eyes of an OWP project developer or investor, it might be also an interesting reading for bankers and lawyers active in the German offshore wind energy sector as well as for students who wish to get more familiar with such red-hot topic.

a better picture of the current market situation in general and possible future developments, as well as to get a practical insight into the mandatory OWP approval process and the recent perceptions and sentiments of banks involved in the financing of OWP in Germany.

1.2 Structure

The following *Section 2* contains definitions of some key terms used throughout this work. Subsequently, a brief illustration of the European and German offshore wind energy market is given to get a better idea of how Germany is currently positioned in this field among its peers.

From an OWP investors' point of view, a stable and supporting political environment considerably reduces the political risks related to such kind of projects, which is usually an important pre-condition for major investments in this field. *Section 3* deals with the political environment OWP project developers or investors are exposed to in Germany and particularly focuses on Germany's offshore wind energy strategy as well as on the German government's recently introduced new energy concept, which is mainly based on renewable energy sources.

In addition, a wise OWP project developer should also be familiar with all relevant legal statutes when planning an OWP and consider all important legal aspects in his project plan accordingly. *Section 4* discusses the legal framework applicable in Germany when intending to realise an OWP in the German EEZ. The main focus is laid on the Renewable Energies Act, RE-Act (*Erneuerbare-Energien-Gesetz, EEG*) and the wind energy priority areas in both the North and the Baltic Sea, which have been defined by the legislator in the course of its spatial planning. Subsequently, this section outlines the mandatory approval process necessary for the realisation of an OWP project, containing, inter alia, references to the relevant legal statutes and a detailed description of each individual approval phase.

The investment volume for a German OWP can easily amount to EUR 1 billion (bn) or more and thus normally requires also a sufficient amount of debt to be injected into the project. Hence, it is also of utmost relevance for an OWP project developer to be very well aware what has to be done to arrange for a project structure which is bankable at the end, in order to be able to secure the debt financing needed. *Section 5* addresses bankability issues related to the realisation of an OWP in the German EEZ and contains an evaluation of the banks' main financing challenges, an outline of applicable banking standards for OWP projects to be considered by the project developer to secure a successful project placement, as well as a brief description of some peculiarities one should be aware of when it comes to granting or taking collateral over assets located in the German EEZ.

Finally, *Section 6* concludes with a summary of the main outcomes and results developed throughout this work.

2. Offshore wind energy in Germany – a pioneer industry in the renewable energy sector

Compared to other renewable energy technologies used in Germany, such as solar technology, the offshore wind energy sector is still in its early development stage. However, the German offshore wind industry has made further progress in the last years despite facing the typical technical and financial challenges when a new technology is trying to establish itself in the market. Installed German offshore wind capacity has continuously grown in the last 2 to 3 years, but is coming from a very low or rather marginal level compared to other European countries like the United Kingdom or Denmark. Nevertheless, one can be certain that offshore wind energy growth rates in Europe and in Germany in particular, will become even stronger in the near future considering the recent political developments after the nuclear disaster in Fukushima (Japan).

Before going into detail, *Section 2.1* defines several key terms used throughout this work. The following *Section 2.2* gives a brief overview about the European and German offshore wind energy market.

2.1 Definitions

2.1.1 Renewable energy and wind energy

Renewable energy is the sustainable production of energy from natural and regenerative resources, such as sunlight, wind or hydro power. Thus, the production of renewable energy is usually very environment-friendly (i.e. low carbon dioxide emissions).[2]

Wind energy is renewable energy/electricity generated from wind by the use of modern windmills (wind generators).

2.1.2 Offshore wind generator and offshore wind park

An offshore wind generator (OWG) is a wind generator which has been erected at least three nautical miles seawards from the coast-line.[3]

The accumulation of several OWG in a certain marine area which are usually under the control of the same operator is called an offshore wind park (OWP).[4]

2.1.3 Territorial Sea

The territorial sea (*Küstenmeer*) of a coastal state is the sea belt adjoining to the coastal state's land territory, which is limited to 12 nautical miles from its coast-line (Territorial Sea or 12-Mile Zone).[5]

2.1.4 Exclusive Economic Zone

The exclusive economic zone (*ausschließliche Wirtschaftszone*) of a coastal state is the sea belt adjoining to the coastal state's Territorial Sea, which is limited to 200 nautical miles from its coast-line (EEZ).[6]

2.2 The European and German (offshore) wind energy market

2.2.1 (Offshore) wind energy in Europe

In 2010, the installed wind energy capacity in the EU totalled 84,074 megawatt (MW), contributing thereby the lion share (43%) to the global wind energy capacity available.[7]

---

2 See Böttcher, Finanzierung von Erneuerbare-Energien-Vorhaben, 2009, p. 9, and Maier, Die Ausdehnung des Raumordnungsgesetzes auf die Ausschließliche Wirtschaftszone (AWZ) dargestellt an der auslösenden Situation der raumordnerischen Steuerung von Offshore-Windenergieanlagen, 2008, p. 2.

3 See Article 3, No. 9 RE-Act (*EEG*). Please note that OWG located closer than three nautical miles from the coast-line are defined as "nearshore". However, the offshore wind industry itself normally does not make use of such differentiation (see Both, Die Rolle der Assekuranz bei der Entwicklung regenerativer Energieformen - am Beispiel der Windenergie in Deutschland, 2006, p. 89).

4 OWP in the German EEZ normally contain 20, 40 or 80 OWG.

5 Simplified definition; for more details, please refer to Part II, Section 1, Article 2 and Section 2, Article 3 et seq. UNCLOS (*SRÜ*).

6 Simplified definition; for more details, please refer to Part V, Article 55 and 57 UNCLOS (*SRÜ*). Maps of the German EEZ for both the Baltic and the North Sea can be found in Appendix F and G respectively.

About 3.5% of that European wind energy capacity (i.e. 2,946 MW) was located offshore, distributed over 9 countries and 45 OWP. In the past, the United Kingdom, Denmark, the Netherlands and Sweden have been the major growth drivers in the European offshore wind energy segment.

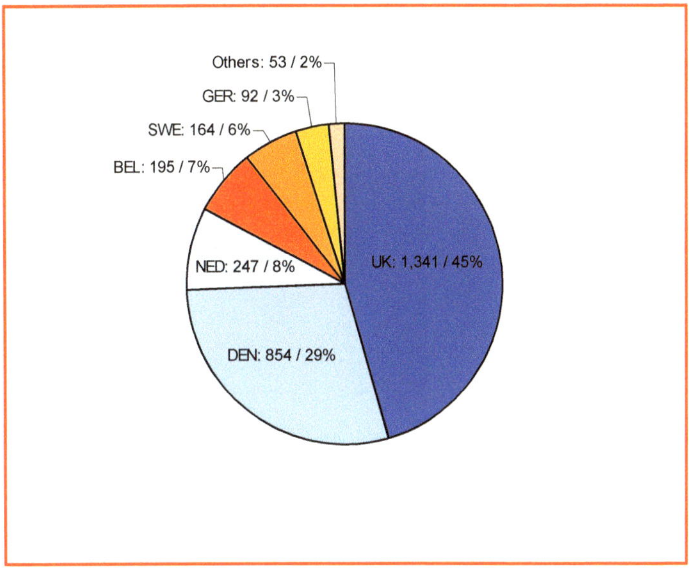

Figure 1: Installed offshore wind capacity (MW)/Cumulative share by country 2010

Source: EWEA, The European offshore wind industry - key trends and statistics 2010

It is not surprising that these countries are also the leading EU member states in terms of total installed offshore wind energy capacity, with the United Kingdom (UK) at the forefront (1,341 MW; 45%) followed by Denmark (DEN) and the Netherlands (NED) with 854 MW (29%) and 247 MW (8%) respectively. The contribution of Germany (GER) to the available European offshore wind energy capacity has so far been rather marginal (2010: 92 MW, 3%) (see Figure 1).

However, a major impact can be expected from German OWP to be erected in the next decade. The German OWP currently under construction will create an additional capacity of about 400 MW and the new German OWP projects, which have already been approved by the German authorities, will provide a capacity of another

---

7 See BMU, Erneuerbare Energien in Zahlen - Nationale und internationale Entwicklung, 2011b, p. 71, http://www.bmu.de/files/pdfs/allgemein/application/ pdf/broschuere_ee_zahlen_bf.pdf (accessed 22 October 2011).

8,435 MW (see Figure 2).[8] In 2020, the total European offshore wind energy capacity is expected to reach a size of 40,000 to 55,000 MW.[9]

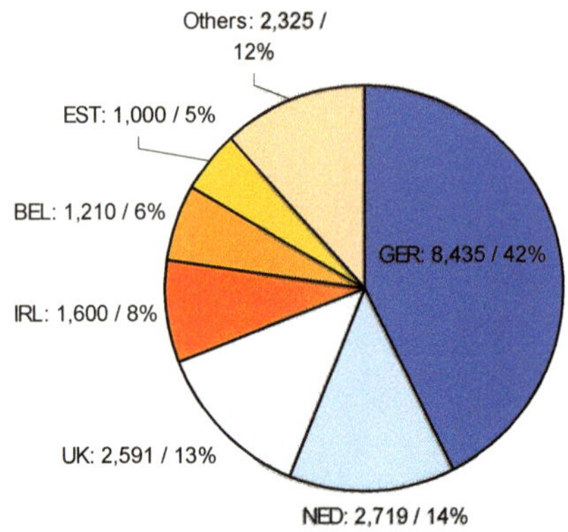

Figure 2: Approved offshore wind capacity (MW)/Cumulative share by country 2010

Source: EWEA, The European offshore wind industry - key trends and statistics 2010

The average size of installed offshore wind turbines in Europe at the end of year 2010 was 3.2 MW, but is very likely to grow further as sizes of up to 5 MW become more and more standard nowadays. The dominating wind turbine suppliers are Siemens AG (Germany) and Vestas Wind Systems A/S (Denmark), covering about 90% of the European offshore wind turbine supply market.[10] The foundation type used is very much depending on the water depth of the sea site where the respective OWP shall be erected.[11]

---

8 See KPMG, Offshore Windparks in Europa - Marktstudie 2010, 2010, p. 19, www.offshore-stiftung.com/Offshore/61/61/60005/.../download.html (accessed 02 October 2011) and EWEA, The European offshore wind industry - key trends and statistics 2010, 2011a, pp. 10-11, 14, http://www.ewea.org/index.php?id=1861 (accessed 22 October 2011).

9 See EWEA, The European offshore wind industry - key trends and statistics 2009, 2010, p. 6, http://www.ewea.org/fileadmin/emag/statistics/2009offshore/pdf/offshore %20stats%2020092.pdf (accessed 22 October 2011).

10 See EWEA, The European offshore wind industry - key trends and statistics 2010, 2011a, p. 12, http://www.ewea.org/index.php?id=1861 (accessed 22 October 2011).

11 Up to 20 m water depth monopile foundations are mainly used (44%), between 20 to 40 m jacket and tripod foundations are rather common (58%), and for water depths of 40 m and more jacket systems are often the preferred choice (49%) (see KPMG, Offshore Windparks in Europa - Marktstudie 2010, 2010, p. 42, www.offshore-stiftung.com/Offshore/61/61/60005/.../

2.2.2 (Offshore) wind energy in Germany

Of the total of 84,074 MW of installed wind energy capacity in the EU, Germany is covering about 27,214 MW (32%), thus holding by far the largest share in Europe and being responsible for the third largest wind energy capacity worldwide after China (42,287 MW) and the United States of America (US) (40,180 MW).[12] In 2010, about 17% of Germany's total electricity consumption (*Stromverbrauch*) has been generated from renewable energy sources[13], whereof electricity produced from wind has contributed the most with 6.2% of the total German electricity supply, followed by biomass (5.5%) and hydro power (3.4%)[14]. The continuous growth of renewable energies helps to reduce greenhouse gases (especially CO_2 emissions) and thus to comply with the international and European climate protection and emission reduction targets, but also, and in particular, to reach the ambitious growth targets defined by the German legislator due to its far-reaching change in energy policy[15]. About 75 million (mn) tons of greenhouse gas emissions have been avoided in 2010 by electricity production from renewable sources, whereof wind energy was responsible for the main part with 27.8 mn tons (37%).[16] Additionally, the wind energy industry, which has created about 100,000 jobs until today, has also become an important

download.html (accessed 02 October 2011)). Overall, the foundation types mostly used so far are monopile (65%) and gravity (25%) structures. However, this might change very soon as water depths and distances to the coast of new European OWP projects are more and more increasing (see EWEA, The European offshore wind industry - key trends and statistics 2010, 2011a, p. 3, http://www.ewea.org/index.php?id=1861 (accessed 22 October 2011)). One of the reasons for this development is that most of the German OWP will be located much further out at sea compared to existing European OWP already operating in compliance with the strict requirements of the German government (if possible no visibility of OWP from the coast). Furthermore, also other European countries are about to develop much more remote marine areas for their offshore wind energy activities (as suitable sites in shorter distances are, to a large extend, already used in this respect).

12 See BMU, Erneuerbare Energien in Zahlen - Nationale und internationale Entwicklung, 2011b, pp. 71-72, http://www.bmu.de/files/pdfs/allgemein/application/ pdf/broschuere_ee_zahlen_bf.pdf (accessed 22 October 2011).

13 The share of electricity supply from renewable sources has continuously grown in Germany over the last 20 years from 3.1% in 1990 to 17.0% in 2010 (see BMU, Erneuerbare Energien in Zahlen - Nationale und internationale Entwicklung, 2011b, p. 13, http://www.bmu.de/files/pdfs/allgemein/application/pdf/broschuere_ee_zahlen_ bf.pdf (accessed 22 October 2011)).

14 See BMU, Development of renewable energy sources in Germany 2010, 2011a, p. 8, http://www.bmu.de/files/english/pdf/application/pdf/ee_in_deutschland_graf_tab_en. pdf (accessed 22 October 2011).

15 See also Sections 3.2.2 and 3.2.3 below.

16 Among all the renewable energies wind energy has the best greenhouse gas avoidance factor (*Treibhausgas-Vermeidungsfaktor*) after hydro power (see BMU, Erneuerbare Energien in Zahlen - Nationale und internationale Entwicklung, 2011b, pp. 24-26, http://www.bmu.de/files/pdfs/allgemein/application/pdf/broschuere_ee_zahlen_bf.pdf (accessed 22 October 2011).

economic factor in Germany over the last years.[17] Despite the aforementioned promising facts referring to the German wind energy sector in general, the offshore wind energy segment in Germany was rather underdeveloped for a long time due to its specific challenges, but is now ready to take off as we will see throughout this work.

But even today the installed German offshore wind energy capacity still amounts only to about 180 MW[18], which is less than 1% of the total German wind energy capacity. Therefore, it is no wonder, that the current contribution of German OWP to the total German electricity consumption is negligible (0.03%)[19]. Nevertheless, considerable and valuable progress has been made in the recent past with the official commissioning (*Inbetriebnahme*) of the Alpha Ventus test site (April 2010) and the first commercial German OWP Baltic 1 (April 2011), as well as with the successful placement of the first pure project finance-based German OWP (Borkum West II) in the banking market (December 2010[20]). All these aspects are positive precedents which will further accelerate the development of the German offshore wind industry in the future. Hence, a strong growth of German offshore wind energy capacity is expected within the next decade. About 10,000 MW shall be available in Germany until 2020, which goes along with an overall investment volume of approximately EUR 30 bn.[21]

Investor groups which have been mainly active in the German offshore wind industry so far are utilities (39%), such as EnBW AG, E.ON AG or RWE AG, independent project developers (28%) and financial investors (e.g. Blackstone Group) (11%) (see Figure 3).[22]

---

17 See BMU, Erneuerbare Energien in Zahlen - Nationale und internationale Entwicklung, 2011b, p. 36, http://www.bmu.de/files/pdfs/allgemein/application/ pdf/broschuere_ee_zahlen_bf.pdf (accessed 22 October 2011).

18 See Appendix D, question 17.

19 See BMU, Erneuerbare Energien in Zahlen - Nationale und internationale Entwicklung, 2011b, p. 12, http://www.bmu.de/files/pdfs/allgemein/application/ pdf/broschuere_ee_zahlen_bf.pdf (accessed 22 October 2011).

20 See Appendix E, question 12.

21 See KPMG, Offshore Windparks in Europa - Marktstudie 2010, 2010, p. 3, www.offshore-stiftung.com/Offshore/61/61/60005/.../download.html (accessed 02 October 2011).

22 See KPMG, Offshore Windparks in Europa - Marktstudie 2010, 2010, p. 54, www.offshore-stiftung.com/Offshore/61/61/60005/.../download.html (accessed 02 October 2011).

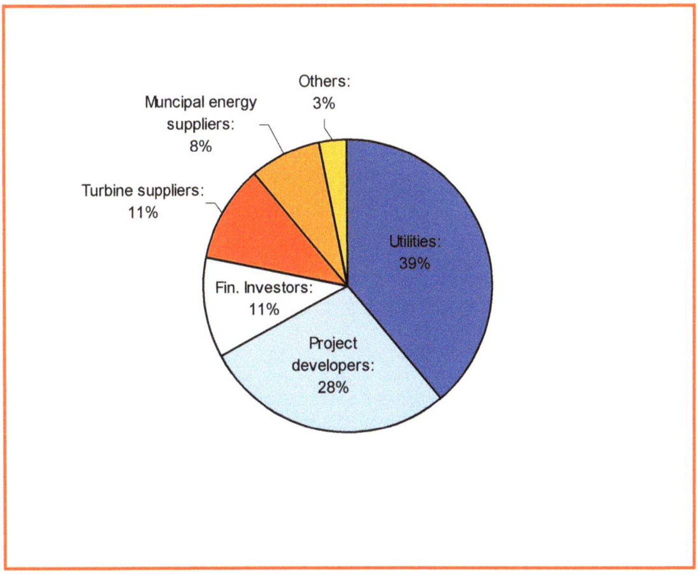

Figure 3: Ownership structure German OWP 2010 (%)

Source: KPMG, Offshore Windparks in Europa - Marktstudie 2010

However, especially the group of financial investors might play a bigger role in the future due to the recent supporting legal changes considered by the German legislator (e.g. improvement of expected return on investment[23]).

Because of the high investment costs related to German OWP[24] and in order to allow nevertheless for an economically feasible operation, average wind turbine sizes used in Germany are normally larger compared to other European countries. The first 5 MW turbines have been erected while suppliers are already developing prototypes with capacities of up to 6 or 7 MW. The German company Siemens AG is the leading supplier for offshore wind turbines in Germany and across Europe.

Despite still being in the early development stage, the German offshore wind industry has made considerable progress in the last 2 to 3 years and is now ready to start a successful growth story, which, however, must be based on a supporting political environment, clear and confidence-building legal statutes as well as the support of the financial industry. The latter must provide sufficient debt finance so that the German

23 See also Section 4.3.

24 German OWP, normally have to cope with larger distances to the coast and higher water depths which cause higher investment costs compared to OWP in other European countries.

offshore wind industry is able to handle the upcoming huge investment volumes in this sector. The German policy measures introduced to promote the offshore wind energy sector will be discussed in detail in the following chapter (*Section 3*). The most relevant legal statutes as well as the challenges related to secure a debt financing for an OWP project in Germany (bankability) are addressed in *Sections 4* and *5* respectively.

3. The political environment for offshore wind energy in Germany

An unexperienced investor might wonder what politics have to do with the successful realisation of an OWP, which seems to be a purely commercial project at first glance. However, in practice a positive political environment, i.e. one which is supportive and reliable, is very important for the success of such kind of projects. This is even more so when technologies in their early development stage, such as the offshore wind energy sector, shall be financed with no recourse to the project sponsors (i.e. by the use of a project finance structure). Hence, a positive attitude of politicians towards the subject matter is essential for many reasons: They can put issues on the political agenda which are important for the offshore wind industry or refrain from doing that, they can be supportive when it comes to the identification of new marine offshore wind energy sites or not, they can arrange for an efficient and fast OWP approval process with less bureaucracy or fail to do that, they can pass encouraging legal reforms (e.g. implement adequate fixed feed-in tariffs)[25] or not, and introduce other supplemental measures supporting the development of the industry[26] or just leave it. Therefore, it should be worthwhile for an OWP investor or project developer to spend at least some time to make himself familiar and comfortable with the respective political environment in the course of his project due diligence.

With its overall energy policy, the German government aims to secure an affordable and reliable energy supply for the industry and private consumers in Germany, strengthen the economy by the development and use of state-of-the-art renewable energy technologies and consequently implement its climate protection targets

25 The legal framework in Germany, including the applicable feed-in tariff scheme, will be discussed in detail in Section 4 below.

26 For example with the implementation of a special offshore wind energy state credit programme as introduced by the German legislator (see Section 3.2.3 for further information).

(*Klimaschutzziele*). However, apart from its own national political goals, the German legislator needs also to consider the requirements of applicable existing international and European agreements as a factor in its policy making, such as the Kyoto Protocol or relevant EU legislation, which are briefly introduced in the following *Section 3.1*.

The subsequent *Section 3.2* describes in more detail the national strategies and policy measures set by the German government. The development and use of renewable energy technologies in general has been promoted by the legislator already since 1990[27]. However, having been a highly risky and unproven technology, for long time the offshore wind energy sector played only a marginal role despite its huge potential. To specifically push the developments in this field, the German government introduced an offshore wind energy strategy in 2002 (Section 3.2.1). Since then further policy measures have been implemented, which, inter alia, had (significant) influence on the offshore wind industry too. The main cornerstones have been the new energy concept of the German government introduced in September 2010 (Section 3.2.2) as well as the additional governmental measures (*Maßnahmenpaket*) passed after the disastrous nuclear accident at the Fukushima power plant in Japan in March 2011 (Section 3.2.3).

3.1 Influence of international and European climate policy

3.1.1 Kyoto Protocol

With the ratification of the internationally applicable Kyoto Protocol to the United Nations Framework Convention on Climate Change ("Kyoto Protocol") passed in 1997, the EU gave a joint binding commitment to reduce greenhouse gas emissions by 8% compared to 1990 levels until 2012[28], which was later distributed between the EU member states by a burden sharing agreement setting the individual reduction target for Germany at 21%[29]. Thus, every EU member state was required to implement adequate measures to be able to comply with its respective emission reduction target. Germany was successful in this respect, by promoting, for example, renewable

---

27 See Section 4.1.1 for further information.

28 See Articles 2, 3 and Annex B of the Kyoto Protocol and Frenz/Müggenborg, Erneuerbare-Energien-Gesetz Kommentar, 2010, pp. 54, 149. The Kyoto Protocol entered into force in 2005 (for further information see BMU, Kyoto Protocol, 2011, pp. 1-2, http://www.bmu.de/english/climate/international_climate_policy/kyoto_ protocol/ doc/41823.php (accessed 29 October 2011)).

29 See Mendonca, Feed-in Tariffs - Accelerating the Development of Renewable Energy, 2007, p. 37.

energy technologies (including the wind energy sector). By the end of 2009, German greenhouse gas emissions had already been reduced by approximately 29% compared to 1990 levels.[30]

3.1.2 Relevant EU legislation

In addition, the EU determined for each member state an individual national target for its respective share of energy from renewable energy sources in gross final energy consumption (*Endenergieverbrauch*) to be reached until 2020. The individual target for Germany was set at 18%.[31] By the end of 2010, Germany reached a share of about 11%[32]. In order to meet the aforementioned target at the end of this decade, Germany has to continue with taking supportive measures and additional efforts. As we will see in the following section, the constant promotion of renewable energies, and the offshore wind energy sector in particular, is one of the main cornerstones of the German government's energy policy to achieve both compliance with its climate protection and emission reduction goals and a successful implementation of its new energy policy (i.e. the transformation of the existing energy mix mainly based on fossil and nuclear sources into an energy mix with its main focus on renewable sources).

3.2 Government policy and support in Germany

3.2.1 Germany's offshore wind energy strategy

The continuous expansion of renewable energies is part of the national sustainability strategy of the German government targeting, inter alia, a more environment-friendly energy supply and a reduction of the dependency on energy imports from other countries. To reach this aim, the legislator has supported the growth of renewable energies already since 1990. Since then, from all renewable energy sources, onshore wind energy has contributed the most to the German energy supply until today[33]. Nevertheless, the German government's intention to continuously maintain the growth of wind energy on a high level proved to be difficult due to the limited

---

30 See BMU, Kyoto Protocol, 2011, pp. 1-2, http://www.bmu.de/english/climate/ international_climate_policy/kyoto_protocol/doc/41823.php (accessed 29 October 2011).

31 See Article 3, No. 1 and Annex 1 of EU Directive 2009/28/EC on the promotion of the use of energy from renewable sources.

32 See BMU, Development of renewable energy sources in Germany 2010, 2011a, p. 2, http://www.bmu.de/files/english/pdf/application/pdf/ee_in_deutschland_graf_tab_en. pdf (accessed 22 October 2011).

33 See Section 2.2.2 above.

number of suitable onshore wind energy sites in Germany. Being aware of this problem and the great offshore wind energy potential in Germany at the same time, the legislator passed its "Strategy of the German Government on the use of off-shore wind energy" (*Strategie der Bundesregierung zur Windenergienutzung auf See*) in 2002 to improve the general conditions (*Rahmenbedingungen*) for the development of the offshore wind industry in Germany. The main elements of this offshore wind energy strategy have been the following:

a) Resolution of existing conflicts between the protection and the use of specific marine areas in Germany;
b) Acceleration of the OWP approval process;
c) Establishment of more legal security and planning reliability for OWP project developers (e.g. by the introduction of particularly suitable areas for OWP in both the North and the Baltic Sea[34]); and
d) Initiation of additional research (e.g. erection of three offshore research platforms in the North and the Baltic Sea).[35]

The introduction of the German offshore wind energy strategy in 2002 was an important turning point for the offshore wind industry in Germany and a first step into the right direction. However, since then additional efforts and political measures have become necessary to overcome the significant technological and other existing challenges related to such pioneer industry sector.

3.2.2 Germany's overall energy concept before Fukushima

In September 2010, the German government published its long-term strategy for the energy supply in Germany until 2050, which shall ensure an effective protection of the climate and the environment, energy security and a fairly priced energy supply.[36]

The main cornerstone of this concept is that renewable energies shall replace fossil and nuclear energy sources step-by-step and contribute the major share to Germany's

[34] For further information see Section 4.2.1.1.

[35] See Bundesregierung, Strategie der Bundesregierung zur Windenergienutzung auf See, 2002, pp. 2, 4, 7, 9-10, 12, 15 et seq., 22, http://www.bmu.de/files/pdfs/allgemein/ application/pdf/windenergie_strategie_br_020100.pdf (accessed 30 October 2011).

[36] See Bundesregierung, Energy Concept for an Environmentally Sound, Reliable, and Affordable Energy Supply (*Energiekonzept für eine umweltschonende, zuverlässige und bezahlbare Energieversorgung*), 2010, p. 3, http://www.bmwi.de/English/ Redaktion/Pdf/energyconcept,property=pdf,bereich=bmwi,sprache=en,rwb=true.pdf (accessed 30 October 2011).

future energy mix.[37] As such a process cannot take place over night nuclear energy was identified to be used as a bridge technology (*Brückentechnolgie*). That is why the legislator at that time extended the operating lives (*Nutzungsdauer*) of all 17 German nuclear power plants in operation by an average of 12 years. As a consequence, the nuclear power plants, which have started operations after 1980, got concession to operate until 2030 or longer.[38]

Furthermore, the German government has defined clear guidelines within its new energy concept to reach its climate protection targets until 2020 (*2050*), which are as follows:

a) Greenhouse gas emissions shall be reduced by a minimum of 40% (*80%*) compared to 1990 levels;

b) Share of electricity generated from renewable energy sources in Germany's total electricity consumption (*Stromverbrauch*) shall account for 35% (*80%*); and

c) Share of energy from renewable energy sources in Germany's gross final energy consumption (*Endenergieverbrauch*) shall increase to 18% (*60%*).

According to the legislator, wind energy plays a key role when it comes to the implementation of such an energy concept, being fully aware of the fact that onshore and offshore wind energy capacities must be extended massively to reach the targeted levels in 2050[39] and that there is further need for (political) action (*Handlungsbedarf*) to achieve that growth. For example, the offshore wind energy capacity of

---

37 Besides the expansion of energy supply from renewable sources, the integrated energy concept of the German government is also aiming at an improvement of energy efficiency, the necessary extension of the onshore electricity grid, as well as at the development of new electricity storage technologies. For further information see Bundesregierung, Energy Concept for an Environmentally Sound, Reliable, and Affordable Energy Supply, 2010, pp. 3-4, 11 et seq., 18 et seq., http://www.bmwi.de/Elish/Redaktion/Pdf/energyconcept,property=pdf,bereich=bmwi,sprache=en, rwb= true.pdf (accessed 30 October 2011).

38 The use of nuclear technology for the production of energy has always been controversially discussed in Germany. After long lasting and intensive debate, the German legislator actually decided already in 2000 to phase out the usage of nuclear power plants over time. However, by the introduction of its new energy concept, such decision has been considerably diluted by the significant extension of the operating lives for German power plants. At that time (i.e. before Fukushima), the German government was of the opinion that such limited extension seemed to be justifiable considering the fact that German nuclear power plants comply with the highest technological standards and belong to the safest in the world (see also Bundesregierung, Energy Concept for an Environmentally Sound, Reliable, and Affordable Energy Supply, 2010, pp. 15-16, http://www.bmwi.de/English/Redaktion/ Pdf/energyconcept,property=pdf,bereich=bmwi,sprache=en,rwb=true.pdf (accessed 30 October 2011).

39 However, new wind energy areas will be rather located offshore. The expected increase of onshore wind capacity will be to a large extent based on repowering activities of existing sites.

25,000 MW to be erected until 2030 alone does require an expected investment volume of about EUR 75 bn.

The identified measures to be implemented in the course of such new energy concept, which are most relevant from the offshore wind industry's point of view, are the following:

a) Introduction of an EUR 5 bn special offshore wind energy state credit programme to accelerate the financing and construction of the first 10 OWP in Germany (elimination of liquidity gap)[40];

b) Applicable legal statutes shall be amended to avoid the hoarding/reservation of licences to build OWP and to streamline the approval process[41];

c) Cost-neutral amendment of applicable feed-in tariffs to facilitate investment in OWP by a higher possible return on investment (introduction of an optional compression model (*Stauchungsmodell*))[42];

d) Update of spatial planning for Germany's EEZ to ensure the availability of sufficient marine sites to cope with the strong expansion of offshore wind energy capacity; and

e) Implementation of a nationwide grid expansion and upgrade plan for the next 10 years to be in the position to process the increasing share of offshore wind energy produced in the North of Germany.[43]

Most of the aforementioned measures have been implemented in the meantime or will become effective in 2011 or as of 01 January 2012 at the latest. Besides the German government's obvious general willingness to continuously support the development of renewable energies, one of the main reasons why the government acted so fast was the nuclear accident in Fukushima which happened in March 2011, i.e. only half a year after the new German energy concept described above had been introduced by the government. Through the nuclear disaster in Japan, the debate about the use of

40 For further information see Section 5.2.2.
41 For further information see Section 4.3.
42 For further information see Section 4.3.
43 See Bundesregierung, Energy Concept for an Environmentally Sound, Reliable, and Affordable Energy Supply, 2010, pp. 4-5, 8-9, http://www.bmwi.de/English/ Redaktion/Pdf/ energyconcept,property=pdf,bereich=bmwi,sprache=en,rwb=true.pdf (accessed 30 October 2011) and Bundesregierung, 10 point immediate action programme (*10-Punkte-Sofortprogramm*), undated/a, pp. 1-2, http://www.bmu.de/files/ pdfs/allgemein/application/pdf/10-punkte-sofortprogramm _en_bf.pdf (accessed 30 October 2011).

nuclear technology in Germany was reopened. The outcome was a complete political turnaround in Germany with regard to nuclear energy, which in consequence put the German legislator under increasing pressure to set up a political environment where renewable energies can flourish as we will see in the following section.

3.2.3 Germany's overall energy concept after Fukushima

The nuclear disaster at the power plant in Fukushima made the world realise that it is impossible, even for one of the highest developed and technological leading countries like Japan, to control the catastrophic impacts of a nuclear accident. The aftermath of Fukushima also had a considerable impact on the energy policy in Germany and caused the German government to reassess its position vis-à-vis the use of nuclear energy and to revaluate the risks related to this kind of technology. Based on this reassessment, the German legislator decided to cancel the extension of the operating lives for German nuclear power plants, which had been passed only half a year earlier. This heavy political turnaround had of course significant effects on the future German energy strategy.

Although this strategy had been already aiming at a strong growth of renewable energies beforehand, the legislator was now forced to improve and supplement its energy strategy even further to arrange for a prosperous environment for alternative energies and to allow for a faster development of such technologies. Indeed, the German government acted very promptly and introduced additional governmental measures (*Maßnahmenpaket*) only about three months after the accident in Fukushima (i.e. in June 2011), which will be reviewed on a yearly basis. The measures most relevant for an OWP investor and/or project developer are as follows:

a) Immediate shutdown of 8 out of 17 German nuclear power plants and phase-out of the remaining 9 nuclear power plants still in operation until 2022[44], which has an enormous positive effect on the future prospects of renewable energy technologies in Germany (with offshore wind energy having the greatest potential);

[44] Thus, the German government has implemented the recommendations of the ethics commission (*Ethik-Kommission*), which was established after the Fukushima nuclear accident to analyse and clarify open questions concerning the future German energy supply in general, but also to suggest a final expiry date for the use of nuclear energy in Germany (see Dreizehntes Gesetz zur Änderung des Atomgesetzes (AtG), http://www.bundesregierung.de/Content/DE/Artikel/2011/08/2011-08-05-gesetze-energiewende.html (accessed 05 November 2011) and Ethik-Kommission, Deutschlands Energiewende - Ein Gemeinschaftswerk für die Zukunft, 2011, pp. 4, 6, http://www.bundesregierung.de/Content/DE/__Anlagen/2011/05/2011-05-30-abschlussbericht-ethikkommission,property=publicationFile.pdf (accessed 05 November 2011).

b) Improvement of feed-in tariff schemes in certain renewable energy sectors where the return on investment has so far been rather insufficient for investors (inter alia, for the offshore wind energy sector)[45];

c) Acceleration of the expansion and upgrading of onshore grids and streamlining of the planning and approval process for nationwide transmission lines (*überregionale Stromleitungen*) to be able to better cope with the growing production of renewable energy in general and especially the necessary transfer from the offshore wind energy production sites in the North of Germany to the main industrialised regions in the South[46];

d) Removal of time limitation of the Transmission System Operators (TSO)' duty to cover all costs related to the OWP' grid connection (i.e. no more uncertainties that these costs may have to be covered by OWP project developers again after the expiry of that legal provision), as well as increased facilitation of smart grids and storage technologies (*Speichertechnologien*) to better cope with the fluctuating energy production by renewable sources (e.g. (offshore) wind energy)[47]; and

e) Faster implementation of some of the measures already identified and agreed in the course of the introduction of the new energy concept shortly before the disaster in Fukushima, such as the establishment of the EUR 5 bn special offshore wind energy state credit programme[48] and the streamlining of the OWP approval

---

45 Before Fukushima the German legislator was looking rather for a cost-neutral way to increase incentives to invest (see Section 3.2.2 above), whereas afterwards also cost increasing measures have been implemented to additionally push the development of renewable energies (e.g. increased feed-in tariff and deferment of tariff reduction scheme for offshore wind energy projects; for further information see Section 4.3 below). Moreover, such supporting measures have been agreed even earlier than initially scheduled, i.e. the corresponding RE-Act amendment (*EEG-Novelle*) has been passed already in 2011 instead of 2012.

46 See also Grid Expansion Acceleration Act, GEAA (*Gesetz über Maßnahmen zur Beschleunigung des Netzausbaus Elektrizitätsnetze*, *NABEG*), http://www.bundes-regierung.de/Content/DE/Artikel/2011/08/2011-08-05-gesetze-energiewende.html (accessed 05 November 2011).

47 See Section 4.3 below and EI-Act (*EnWG*) amendment (*Gesetz zur Neuregelung energiewirtschaftsrechtlicher Vorschriften, EnWGÄndG*), http://www.Bundes-regierung.de/Content/DE/Artikel/2011/08/2011-08-05-gesetze-energiewende.html (accessed 05 November 2011).

48 This programme has been introduced by the German state bank "Kreditanstalt für Wiederaufbau (KfW)" in the meantime (program no. 273 - Offshore-Windenergie - was released in June 2011) and allows for a direct participation of KfW in loans and/or cost overrun facilities of up to 50% per OWP project, however, with an upper limit of EUR 400 mn and EUR 100 mn respectively. The maximum life of such loans is 20 years with grace periods of up to 3 years. For further information see KfW, Merkblatt KfW-Programm Offshore-Windenergie, 2011, http://k-f-w.net/kfw/de/I/II/Download_ Center/Foerderprogramme/versteckter_Ordner_fuer_PDF/6000001940_M_273_ Offshore_Windenergie.pdf (accessed 30 October 2011).

process to further accelerate the development of the offshore wind energy sector.[49]

After the nuclear accident in Fukushima and the decision to phase out the use of nuclear power plants in Germany much faster, the legislator has shown once again its willingness to strongly support the development of renewable energies by the quick implementation of effective and supportive measures. In particular the offshore wind industry faces a very supporting and stable political environment in Germany. One can barely find precedents in the past where the legislator has supported a subject matter in such a sustainable way[50] and has continuously improved and adjusted the political framework when necessary, which is very likely to be the case also in the future[51].

3.3 Chapter summary and outlook

Implementing the complete phase-out of nuclear energy in Germany until 2022 on the one hand, while complying with the legislator's main target to secure an affordable and reliable energy supply on the other hand, will be the major challenge for German policy makers in the future. As already demonstrated above, a lot of supportive and effective governmental measures have been passed and implemented in the (recent) past to accelerate the growth of renewable energies in Germany, which is very likely to be the case also in the future when the German legislator deems it necessary.

---

49 See BMWi, Der Weg zur Energie der Zukunft - sicher, bezahlbar und umweltfreundlich, 2011a, pp. 1 et seq., http://www.bmwi.de/BMWi/Navigation/ energie,did=405004.html (accessed 05 November 2011).

50 No matter which political party was running the country.

51 In October 2010, German environment minister Röttgen said: "We will only be able to meet our energy policy target of 25,000 megawatt offshore wind power by 2030 if we resolutely advance the expansion of this energy sector. […]". So, prospects are good that the German offshore wind energy industry can continue to rely on a supporting political environment (see BMU, EU Commission approves state aid for offshore wind farm alpha ventus - Environment Minister Röttgen noted: Decision comes at the right time, 2010, p. 1, http://www.bmu.de/ english/current_press_releases/pm/46658.php (accessed 29 October 2011)).

Political environment for offshore wind energy in Germany: major milestones		
Offshore wind energy strategy (2002):	**Energy concept before Fukushima (2010):**	**Energy concept after Fukushima (2011):**
- Improvement of general conditions for the development of offshore wind energy to maintain high growth of wind energy; - Solution of conflict between the protection and use of marine areas; - Acceleration of OWP approval process; - Establishment of particularly suitable areas for OWP (which became later even offshore wind energy priority areas); - Initiation of additional research.	- Future energy mix shall be mainly based on renewable sources with the use of nuclear energy as bridge technology (extension of operating lives); - Introduction of an offshore wind energy state credit programme; - Cost-neutral amendment of feed-in tariffs to increase incentives to invest in German OWP; - Update of spatial planning for German EEZ; - Further streamlining of OWP approval process; - Implementation of onshore grid expansion plan.	- Revaluation of nuclear technology (immediate shutdown of 8 nuclear power plants and faster phase-out of the remaining 9 power plants until 2022); - Increased focus on renewable energies and offshore wind energy in particular; - Considerable improvement of feed-in tariffs for OWP to attract investment; - Faster implementation of previously identified supporting measures (e.g. state credit programme, streamlining approval process, acceleration of onshore grid expansion); - Removal of time limitation of TSO' duty to cover OWP grid connection costs.

Figure 4: Political environment for offshore wind energy in Germany

Overall, the legislator has laid a very solid, reliable and encouraging political foundation for the continuous and strong growth of renewable energies in Germany, but, in particular, for the development of the offshore wind energy sector (see Figure 4), which is considered to be the major source of renewable energy in Germany in the future. It is now up to the sponsors, the financial industry, and of course the project developers themselves to make use of such a supporting political environment and to facilitate the transformation from a nuclear and fossil-based German energy supply to an energy supply mainly based on renewable sources.

4. Legal framework and approval process for the construction of OWP in the German EEZ

The previous chapter has demonstrated that OWP project developers face positive political sentiment and a supporting political environment in Germany. However, even more important for the successful realisation of a German OWP is a precise knowledge of the legal framework applicable to be able to consider all relevant aspects in the project planning. Hence, the legal statutes most relevant for an OWP project developer will be discussed in *Section 4.1*. Furthermore, the erection of an OWP in Germany is subject to approval by the relevant authorities. A good knowledge of the requirements of the authorities involved and its procedures is therefore necessary to allow for a fast and efficient approval process and to avoid or at least minimize costly delays of the erection of the respective OWP. The legal basis of this approval process as well as the individual approval phases an OWP project planner has to go through are described in *Section 4.2*.

4.1 Legal framework

The by far most important legal statute when it comes to the realisation of an OWP in Germany is the RE-Act (*EEG*), which will be discussed in detail in the following *Section 4.1.1*. The subsequent *Section 4.1.2* briefly outlines some complementing provisions considered in the Energy Industry Act, EI-Act (*Energiewirtschaftsgesetz, EnWG*) of which an OWP project developer should be aware of too.

4.1.1 Renewable Energies Act

In 1990, the German government has started to aid the development of renewable energies with the introduction of its first feed-in law (*Stromeinspeisungsgesetz*), which was continuously enhanced and finally replaced by the introduction of the RE-Act (*EEG*) in 2000. Since then, two RE-Act amendments (*EEG-Novellen*) were passed in the years 2004 and 2009 respectively to correspond to the fast development of the renewable energy sector, of which the latter is still in force today.[52]

A precise knowledge of the provisions of the RE-Act (*EEG*) and the applicable mechanisms is vital for potential investors and/or project developers when pursuing an OWP project in Germany.

The following remarks will focus on the RE-Act (*EEG*) articles and complementary matters which should be most relevant to OWP investors when thinking about an investment in a German OWP. They include, a brief description of the purpose of the RE-Act (*EEG*), a detailed explanation of TSO' duties vis-à-vis OWP operators (*Anlagenbetreiber*) and an assessment of the reliability of the existing legal set-up in Germany, i.e. whether investors' confidence in the legal statutes applicable is protected (*Vertrauensschutz*). Finally, a short evaluation of the effectiveness and competitiveness of the overall German feed-in system is conducted.

---

[52] A third RE-Act amendment (*EEG-Novelle*) has already been passed by the German government in year 2011 to further push the development of renewable energy and the area of offshore wind energy in particular. Such amendment will enter into force as of 01 January 2012 and thus one year earlier than initially scheduled. The major changes compared to the currently applicable legislation are outlined in Section 4.3 below. The RE-Act (*EEG*) is a typical feed-in tariff model, the most successful support scheme used by policy makers so far to support the growth of renewable energy (for further details concerning the specifics of a feed-in tariff model and the beginnings of the overall development of the German feed-in law system see Mendonca, Feed-in Tariffs - Accelerating the Development of Renewable Energy, 2007, pp. XIV, 8-9, 13 and 26 et seq.).

4.1.1.1 *Purpose of the RE-Act (EEG)*

The main purpose of the RE-Act (*EEG*) is the protection of the climate and the environment[53], the security and sustainability of energy supply as well as the promotion of renewable energy sources, which also includes the erection of OWP in the German EEZ.[54] With the implementation of the latest amendment of this act in 2009 being still in force today, the German government ambitiously aimed to increase the share of renewable energy to at least 30% of the total German electricity supply in 2020.[55] The German RE-Act (*EEG*) is one of the leading feed-in laws worldwide and shall provide potential investors in renewable energy projects in Germany as much planning reliability and investment security as possible. It, inter alia, establishes a clear and certain regulation of the relationship between TSO and OWP operators by stipulating far reaching TSO duties to support the activities of the offshore wind energy industry.[56]

4.1.1.2 *TSO duties*

To attract investments in the field of renewable energy in Germany, the RE-Act (*EEG*) grants OWP operators certain rights providing for additional comfort when making an investment decision. These rights are basically structured as clearly defined duties the respective TSO has to comply with when dealing with a specific OWP operator (*Netzbetreiberpflichten*).

The main duties are the requirement to connect the OWP with the onshore grid, to purchase, transmit and distribute the energy generated by the respective OWP, the remuneration of the offshore wind energy fed in to the grid (payment of feed-in tariff) and to expand grid capacity if needed. These duties are described in the following in more detail:

---

53 The German RE-Act (*EEG*) was, inter alia, designed to set up a national legal framework accelerating the compliance with the binding international and European climate protection and greenhouse gas reduction targets mentioned already above (see also Sections 3.1.1 and 3.1.2).

54 See Articles 1, 2 No. 1, 3 No. 3 and No. 9 RE-Act (*EEG*).

55 See Articles 1 (2) RE-Act (*EEG*). Such share has been increased to 35% in the meantime in the course of the introduction of Germany's new energy strategy in September 2010 (see Section 3.2.2 above) and will be adjusted in the course of the next amendment of the RE-Act (*EEG*) accordingly (see Article 1 (2) No. 1, Bundesregierung, Gesetz für den Vorrang Erneuerbarer Energien (Erneuerbare-Energien-Gesetz - EEG), Konsolidierte (unverbindliche) Fassung des Gesetzestextes in der ab 1. Januar 2012 geltenden Fassung, undated/c, http://www.bmu.de/ files/pdfs/allgemein/ application/pdf/eeg_2012_bf.pdf (accessed 11 September 2011)).

56 Please note that even though Section 4.1.1 of this work usually specifically refers to OWP projects or OWP operators, most of the relevant articles of the RE-Act (*EEG*) do apply to renewable energy projects in general.

a) Duty to connect *(Anschlusspflicht)*: As indicated above, TSO are required to connect OWP immediately and with priority to their respective grids.[57] In case a TSO should not comply with that duty by willful misconduct and/or negligence (*vorsätzliches Missverhalten und/oder schuldhafte Fahrlässigkeit*), the respective OWP operator concerned is entitled to claim for damages (*Schadensersatzanspruch*).[58] At least of same importance as the implementation of a successful and timely grid connection itself is the question, who will bear the considerable costs caused by such a measure. Normally, those costs would have to be borne by the OWP operator itself.[59] However, having the necessary boost of offshore wind energy in mind to meet its ambitious growth targets, the German legislator has considered a special regime for the grid connection of OWP erected in the German EEZ, which exceptionally requires that the respective TSO has to cover any costs related to it[60].

b) Duty to purchase, transmit and distribute (*Pflicht zur Abnahme, Übertragung und Verteilung*): Besides covering the costs for the establishment of the OWP grid connection, the TSO is also obliged to purchase, transmit and distribute the entire electricity which is offered to it by an OWP operator. Again, the TSO has to comply with that duty immediately and has to give electricity generated by renewable sources priority vis-à-vis electricity produced from conventional sources.[61]

c) Duty to remunerate (*Vergütungspflicht*): When feeding in his offshore wind energy into a TSO grid, the OWP operator receives a claim for payment from the respective TSO, who in turn has to remunerate the OWP operator in line with the

---

57 See Article 5 (1) RE-Act (*EEG*).

58 The Articles 276 and 280 of the German Civil Code, GCC (*Bürgerliches Gesetzbuch, BGB*) would apply accordingly (for further information see Frenz/Müggenborg, Erneuerbare-Energien-Gesetz Kommentar, 2010, p. 272 and Gabler, EEG 2009 - Grundzüge der neuen Rechtslage für Anlagen- und Netzbetreiber: Netzanschluss, Einspeisung, Vergütung, Ausgleichsregelung, Rechtsschutz, 2010, pp. 21-22).

59 See Article 13 (1) RE-Act (*EEG*).

60 For more details please refer to the subsequent Section 4.1.2 covering the relevant complementary provisions of the EI-Act (*EnWG*).

61 See Article 8 (1) RE-Act (*EEG*). The priority principle (*Vorrangprinzip*) applicable in Article 5 and 8 RE-Act (*EEG*) shall give energy from renewable sources a preferential treatment compared to energy from conventional sources (fossil or nuclear energy). That means that, for example, in cases of limited grid capacity, conventional energy operators would have to reduce their amounts of electricity produced to allow for a complete feed-in of the renewable energy available (see BMU, EEG - Das Erneuerbare Energien Gesetz: Die Erfolgsgeschichte nachhaltiger Politik für den Standort Deutschland, 2007, p. 5 and Gabler, EEG 2009 - Grundzüge der neuen Rechtslage für Anlagen- und Netzbetreiber: Netzanschluss, Einspeisung, Vergütung, Ausgleichsregelung, Rechtsschutz, 2010, pp. 13-14).

requirements of the RE-Act (*EEG*).[62] The RE-Act (*EEG*) remuneration scheme for offshore wind energy consists of a basic tariff (*Grundvergütung*), an initial tariff (*Anfangsvergütung*), the commencement and duration of the respective tariff payment (*Vergütungsbeginn und -dauer*) and an applicable tariff/bonus reduction scheme (*Absenkung von Vergütungen und Boni bzw. Degression*).[63]

The basic tariff for offshore wind energy in general is currently fixed at EUR 3.5 cents per kilowatt-hour (kwh).[64]

The applicable initial tariff amounts to EUR 13.0 cents per kwh and can increase by another EUR 2.0 cents per kwh if the OWP, or, to be more precise, the respective offshore wind generator (OWG) has reached its commissioning stage (*Inbetriebnahme*) before 01 January 2016 (increased initial tariff/*erhöhte Anfangsvergütung* or *"Sprinterprämie"*).

The payment of the initial tariff as outlined above is limited to a duration of 12 years. Such period shall be extended by 0.5 months for each full nautical mile a respective OWG is located beyond the 12-Mile Zone and by 1.7 months for each additional full meter of water depth beyond 20 meters.[65] If the payment period of the initial tariff has expired, the basic tariff will be applied until the final expiry date of the feed-in scheme, which is 20 years plus the remaining year when the commissioning stage for the OWG has been reached.[66] The OWP operator has the right to receive payment from the TSO as outlined above, once the respective OWG produces electricity exclusively from renewable sources and such electricity is fed into the grid system.[67]

---

62 See Article 16 (1) RE-Act (*EEG*) in connection with Articles 20 (1), (2) No. 7, 21 and 31 (1), (2). Alternatively, an OWP operator also has the opportunity to sell the energy produced directly to third parties (Direct selling/*Direktvermarktung*) (see Article 17 (1) RE-Act (*EEG*)).

63 Based on Frenz/Müggenborg, Erneuerbare-Energien-Gesetz Kommentar, 2010, pp. 672 et seq.

64 See Article 31 (1) RE Act (*EEG*).

65 See Article 31 (2) RE-Act (*EEG*). Please note that those rules will apply for each individual generator of an OWP separately, i.e. the remuneration of a whole OWP will be calculated for each of its wind turbines individually. A good example how the remuneration scheme of the RE-Act (*EEG*) works in detail can be found in Frenz/Müggenborg, Erneuerbare-Energien-Gesetz Kommentar, 2010, p. 675.

66 See Article 21 (2) RE-Act (*EEG*).

67 See Article 21 (1) RE-Act (*EEG*). At first glance, the concurrence of Article 21 (1) and (2) RE-Act (*EEG*) sounds very plausible. However, the legislator has made a very fine distinction between the *commencement date* of the remuneration period on the one hand (Article 21 (1): first commissioning of OWG - no matter whether by pure renewable energy or not, an available grid connection and thus possible feed-in is not necessary for such purpose), and the *moment* when the OWP operator really has a *claim for payment* on the other (Article 21 (2): production of electricity exclusive-

For all the aforementioned offshore wind energy tariffs, a tariff/bonus reduction scheme applies considering a tariff reduction of 5% per year (degression) starting in 2015.[68] The legislator has introduced this concept in expectation of lower future production costs for offshore equipment (e.g. economies of scale) and other learning curve effects by OWP suppliers and operators. Furthermore, such a mechanism shall also secure the continuous public support of the development of renewable energies, as sky-high returns for OWP investors to be finally paid by the public could negatively affect the positive attitude towards this kind of renewable energy.

d) Duty to expand grid capacity (*Pflicht zur Erweiterung der Netzkapazität*): Temporary shortages of grid capacity (e.g. due to an oversupply of electricity) could have harmful negative effects on the economics of an OWP project, as the electricity produced cannot be fed into the grid and thus the OWP operators' payment claim would be lost during this period. However, to arrange for further OWP investors' certainty, the legislator has obliged the TSO to continuously optimise, improve and even extend its grids, if necessary, to allow for a smooth electricity transmission from the OWP to the onshore grids and thereafter. The OWP operator has the right to claim damages in case the TSO should not comply with that duty by purpose or by negligence.[69]

e) Other TSO duties: Further duties of TSO, such as information and publication requirements, are also considered in the RE-Act (*EEG*), but are less relevant for potential OWP investors.[70]

In summary, the legislator has stipulated very far reaching rights for OWP operators in the RE-Act (*EEG*) to support the development of the offshore wind energy sector in Germany, by requiring the respective TSO to comply with quite a number of binding duties vis-à-vis OWP operators.

---

ly from renewable sources and successful feed-in into the grid system as already mentioned above) (see also Gabler, EEG 2009 - Grundzüge der neuen Rechtslage für Anlagen- und Netzbetreiber: Netzanschluss, Einspeisung, Vergütung, Ausgleichsregelung, Rechtsschutz, 2010, pp. 96-97). Hence, OWP operators should facilitate that commissioning (*Inbetriebnahme*) of its OWG will take place only shortly before or only when the respective grid connection is available to avoid a partial loss of its payment claim (see also Kersting, Die Projektfinanzierung eines Offshore-Windparks, 2011, p. 59).

68 See Article 20 (1) No. 7a RE-Act (*EEG*).

69 See Article 9 (1) and 10 (1) RE-Act (*EEG*).

70 A detailed overview of all TSO duties considered in the RE-Act (*EEG*) can be found in Frenz/Müggenborg, Erneuerbare-Energien-Gesetz Kommentar, 2010, pp. 243 et seq.

4.1.1.3 Protection of investors' confidence

As indicated above, the RE-Act (*EEG*) gives energy generated from renewable sources a preferential treatment compared to energy produced from conventional sources. A wise OWP operator or investor should therefore ask the question whether the German feed-in system is in line with existing EU regulation (e.g. the prohibition of state aid (*Beihilfeverbot*) and/or the principle of free movement of goods (*Warenverkehrsfreiheit*)). The answer is: Yes. The European Court of Justice decided that the German feed-in model to support the development of renewable energy does not violate applicable European law[71], which gives OWP investors the comfort that the content of the German RE-Act (*EEG*) cannot be questioned from a European law perspective.

However, once the investment has been made, an OWP operator could still face the theoretical risk that the national legislator in Germany may subsequently adjust or amend the applicable feed-in system and that the resulting new regulation would have a negative effect on the economics of his project (the most obvious example would be the potential risk of a reduction of the applicable feed-in tariffs).[72] In practice, such a risk is rather remote. German legal experts agree that OWP investors should be protected by the German legal system from subsequent adverse changes of the RE-Act (*EEG*)[73] and can usually rely on the legal environment which was applicable when making their investment decision. Furthermore, the German legislator is very much aware of the fact that such a tremendous legal and/or financial risk would

[71] See Gabler, EEG 2009 - Grundzüge der neuen Rechtslage für Anlagen- und Netzbetreiber: Netzanschluss, Einspeisung, Vergütung, Ausgleichsregelung, Rechtsschutz, 2010, pp. 7-8, Frenz/Müggenborg, Erneuerbare-Energien-Gesetz Kommentar, 2010, p. 85, and Oschmann/Sösemann, Erneuerbare Energien im deutschen und europäischen Recht - Ein Überblick, 2007, p. 2.

[72] Indeed, the implementation of the first and second RE-Act amendment (*EEG-Novellen*), a third one under way, indicates that the legal environment may change from time to time. However, so far the legislator has only reacted on new developments not yet considered in the relevant statutes and usually always improved conditions for OWP investors to further increase incentives for investments in the offshore wind energy sector.

[73] Klinski comes to the conclusion that investors should be in general protected from subsequent legal changes, but names two exemptions: The first one, the existence of a contradictory EU regulation, is rather theoretical, as German legislation is in line with existing EU law, and it is rather unlikely that the EU will issue a directive which could have a potential negative effect on the development of renewable energies in the future. The second exemption is that the German legislator might have the right to reduce feed-in tariffs if it should turn out that the initial levels set were too high and OWP investors gain an inappropriate high return on their investment which is much higher than initially expected by the state and the OWP operator/investor (see Klinski, EEG-Vergütung: Vertrauensschutz bei künftigen Änderungen der Rechtslage?, 2009, pp. 45 et seq.). However, the potential risk of OWP investors to "lose" an upside which they never really expected to occur should not hinder a rational investor to invest.

barely be acceptable for potential investors and accordingly would constrain the targeted strong expansion of the German renewable energy sector.

Hence, OWP investors in Germany can rely on a very stable and supporting legal environment (protection of investors' confidence (*Vertrauensschutz*)) and should have enough legal certainty to invest in the German renewable energy sector and the offshore wind energy segment in particular.

4.1.1.4 Evaluation of German RE-Act (EEG)

In his work, Mendonca has analysed different renewable energy support schemes worldwide as well as varying feed-in laws, and deduced general lessons and requirements for the effective implementation of a feed-in law. The main aspects are to set up a simple, flexible and transparent feed-in system, to guarantee grid connection and a fixed feed-in tariff which is high enough to ensure a profitable operation, to differentiate between different types of renewable energies, and finally to assure public support and acceptance.[74]

Indeed, the German RE-Act (*EEG*) considers all the aforementioned requirements for an effective feed-in law and thus provides investors in renewable energy projects in Germany an environment with high investment security and planning reliability. Furthermore, the German public has always supported the development of alternative and "green" energies in the past and will do so even more after the nuclear accident at the Fukushima power plant in Japan.

If well-designed and implemented, a feed-in model like the German RE-Act (*EEG*) has proven to be the most effective and successful instrument to support and accelerate the development of renewable energies. A positive development of renewable energies can usually be achieved much faster and cheaper compared to alternative models like the UK quota model.[75] The German feed-in law is one of the most successful in the world.[76] Similar feed-in systems have been introduced subsequently

---

74 See Mendonca, Feed-in Tariffs - Accelerating the Development of Renewable Energy, 2007, pp. 103-104.

75 See Mendonca, Feed-in Tariffs - Accelerating the Development of Renewable Energy, 2007, pp. XIV et seq., XX, 16 et seq. and 13 for the pros and cons of feed-in laws.

76 The introduction of the RE-Act (*EEG*) has led to a significant increase of the share of renewable energies in total German electricity consumption from 6% in 2000 to 17% in 2010 (see Bundesregierung, Entwurf - Erfahrungsbericht 2011 zum Erneuerbare-Energien-Gesetz (EEG-Erfahrungsbericht), 2011, p. 3, http://www.bmu.de/files/pdfs/ allgemein/application/ pdf/eeg_erfahrungsbericht_2011_entwurf.pdf (accessed 11 September 2011)).

in many other countries in Europe, but also in countries outside Europe like India or China.[77]

4.1.2 Energy Industry Act

Besides a good knowledge of the content of the RE-Act (*EEG*), an OWP investor should also be aware of some important complementing provisions contained in the German EI-Act (*EnWG*). The main purpose of the EI-Act (*EnWG*) is to secure for the general public a reliable, reasonably priced, environment-friendly and efficient energy supply, which also includes the TSO' duties to expand the grids if necessary and to continuously provide for the grid capacity needed.[78] When it comes to the realisation of an OWP, the EI-Act (*EnWG*) contains two relevant and interrelated provisions[79], both dealing with the TSO' duty to establish the necessary grid connection, which will be discussed in the following in more detail:

- Duty to connect to grid (*Netzanschlusspflicht*) and to cover the related costs (*Kostenübernahme*): As indicated in the previous section, which has covered the provisions of the RE-Act (*EEG*) most relevant for OWP operators, TSO are required to connect OWP to be erected in the German EEZ with the onshore grid, but the respective OWP operator usually would have to compensate for the related costs caused.[80] However, to further boost the development of the promising offshore wind energy sector, the German legislator has introduced an exemption from that regulation in 2006[81], which was later incorporated as an amendment to the EI-Act (*EnWG*). According to the new provision, TSO are not only required to connect OWP/OWG until the date of its technical operational readiness (*technische Betriebsbereitschaft*) at the latest, but also to bear the complete costs caused by the grid connection.[82] However, OWP operators and potential investors should consider

77 See BMU, EEG - Das Erneuerbare Energien Gesetz: Die Erfolgsgeschichte nachhaltiger Politik für den Standort Deutschland, 2007, pp. 20-21.

78 See Articles 1 (1), 11(1) and 12 (3) EI-Act (*EnWG*).

79 See Article 17 (2a) in connection with 118 (3) EI-Act (*EnWG*).

80 See Articles 5 (1) and 13 (1) RE-Act (*EEG*).

81 The relevant provision was part of the Infrastructure Planning Acceleration Act, IPAA (*Infrastrukturplanungsbeschleunigungsgesetz, InfraStrPlanVBeschlG*) which was passed in 2006.

82 The introduction of this cost exemption provision has had a significant positive effect on the profitability of OWP in Germany, as TSO now would have to cover the respective grid connection costs which so far have been responsible for about one third of the total investment costs for an OWP (see Dena, Offshore-Netze - Die Netzanbindung der Offshore-Windparks, 2009, pp. 1-2, http://www.dena.de/themen/ thema-esd/publikationen/publikation/dena-factsheet-offshore-netze-die-netzanbindung-der-offshore-windparks/ (accessed 09 September 2011).

that this exceptional rule does only apply to OWP/OWG whose construction has commenced on or before 31 December 2015.[83]

However, despite the existence of the above regulation, in practice a lot of uncertainties and problems between OWP operators and TSO could be observed in the past. Most of the OWP operating to date have faced (considerable) delays until the respective grid connection was in place. That is why the German Federal Network Agency, GFNA (*Bundesnetzagentur, BNetzA*) has published a clarifying position paper to further improve legal, planning and investment security for OWP operators and investors.

The GFNA (*BNetzA*) position paper (*Positionspapier zur Netzanbindungsverpflichtung gemäß § 17 Abs. 2a EnWG*[84]) contains the requirement that an OWP project developer must adequately and sufficiently demonstrate that his respective OWP project will materialize (*hinreichender Nachweis der Realisierungswahrscheinlichkeit*) to avoid any unnecessary costs of the TSO responsible for the erection of the respective grid connection.[85] In order to provide this evidence, an OWP developer should comply with the following criteria for grid connection (*Anbindungskriterien*) defined by the GFNA (*BNetzA*):

1) Availability of all necessary authorisations (*öffentliche Genehmigungen*) necessary for the erection of the OWP (the approval to be granted by the Federal Maritime and Hydrographic Agency, FMHA (*Bundesamt für Seeschifffahrt und Hydrographie, BSH*) in particular[86]);

---

83 See Article 17 (2a) in connection with 118 (3) EI-Act (*EnWG*). These two specific offshore wind energy-related articles do prevail over the general provisions considered in Article 5 and 13 (1) of the RE-Act (*EEG*) (see Gabler, EEG 2009 - Grundzüge der neuen Rechtslage für Anlagen- und Netzbetreiber: Netzanschluss, Einspeisung, Vergütung, Ausgleichsregelung, Rechtsschutz, 2010, p. 58, and Frenz/Müggenborg, Erneuerbare-Energien-Gesetz Kommentar, 2010, p. 404). Furthermore, legal experts are of the opinion that the TSO right to refuse the establishment of a grid connection, if economically unreasonable (*unzumutbar*) according to Article 17 (2) EI-Act (*EnWG*), does not apply under the offshore wind energy-specific Article 17 (2a) EI-Act (*EnWG*). However, even if the general Article 17 (2) EI-Act (*EnWG*) would apply, TSO would probably have difficulties to provide such evidence as they usually can pass on all related costs to the end customers (see Britz/Hellermann/Hermes, EnWG - Energiewirtschaftsgesetz, 2010, pp. 200, 265).

84 See BNetzA, Positionspapiers zur Netzanbindungsverpflichtung gemäß § 17 Abs. 2a EnWG, 2009, http://www.bundesnetzagentur.de/DE/Sachgebiete/ElektrizitaetGas/ Sonderthemen/AnbindungOffshoreWindparks/AnbindungOffshoreWindparks_node. html (accessed 09 September 2011).

85 See BNetzA, Positionspapier zur Netzanbindungsverpflichtung gemäß § 17 Abs. 2a EnWG, 2009, p. 4, http://www.bundesnetzagentur.de/DE/Sachgebiete/ElektrizitaetGas /Sonderthemen/AnbindungOffshoreWindparks/AnbindungOffshoreWindparks_node. html (accessed 09 September 2011).

86 Please refer to the subsequent Section 4.2 for further information.

2) Provision of a feasible time schedule (*Bauzeitenplan*) containing a description of the major construction stages (*wesentliche Bauabschnitte*);
3) Availability of ground investigation (*Baugrunduntersuchung*) of respective OWP site; and
4) Availability of binding wind turbine supply contracts (*verbindliche Verträge über die Bestellung der Windenergieanlagen*) in connection with a) the evidence that the financing for the OWP has been secured (*verbindliche Finanzierung*), i.e. availability of investors' capital as well as of the necessary bank debt commitments, or, alternatively, b) the availability of "pre"-supply or reservation contracts (*Reservierungs-vereinbarungen*) for the main large components (*Großkomponenten*) of the respective OWP, such as the foundations and the transformer station/platform.

The TSO has the duty to provide to the OWP operator a conditional grid connection undertaking (*bedingte Netzanbindungszusage*) if either the aforementioned grid connection criteria no. 1 to 3, or, alternatively, criteria no. 1, 2 and 4 have been satisfied by the respective OWP operator. In case all four criteria have been met, an unconditional grid connection undertaking (*unbedingte Netzanbindungszusage*) must be issued by the TSO. Furthermore, the TSO is required to arrange for the necessary grid connection as soon as reasonable possible, but within 30 months after the issuance of the conditional grid connection undertaking at the latest.[87]

In case of a delayed grid connection, the OWP operator has the right to claim damages if the TSO has behaved unreasonably.[88] So, an OWP operator is protected in case a TSO has shown wilful misconduct and/or negligence, whereas to date no damages can be claimed in cases where a delayed grid connection was the result of unexpected matters the TSO could not foresee despite acting reasonably (i.e. acts of god/force majeure[89], such as bad weather conditions at sea). But the fact that risks related to

---

87 See BNetzA, Positionspapiers zur Netzanbindungsverpflichtung gemäß § 17 Abs. 2a EnWG, 2009, pp. 5 et seq., http://www.bundesnetzagentur.de/DE/Sachgebiete/ Elektrizitaet/ Gas/Sonderthemen/AnbindungOffshoreWindparks/AnbindungOffshore Windparks _node.html (accessed 09 September 2011).

88 See Kersting, Die Projektfinanzierung eines Offshore-Windparks, 2011, p. 59, Gabler, EEG 2009 - Grundzüge der neuen Rechtslage für Anlagen- und Netzbetreiber: Netzanschluss, Einspeisung, Vergütung, Ausgleichsregelung, Rechtsschutz, 2010, p. 60, Britz/Hellermann/Hermes, EnWG - Energiewirtschaftsgesetz, 2010, pp. 200, 265 and Wustlich, Das Recht der Windenergie im Wandel - Teil 2: Windenergie auf See, 2007, p. 128.

89 For further information regarding the force majeure concept in general see Vinter, Project Finance, 1998, pp. 88 et seq.

force majeure are normally not covered in (project) financings is also true for other industries.[90] Hence, an OWP investor should consider the potential risk of a delayed grid connection when planning an OWP project (i.e. the planning should include a reasonable time buffer).

Overall, the issuance of the GFNA (*BNetzA*) position paper has considerably reduced investors' uncertainties and thus clearly improved planning reliability for OWP in Germany.

Legal framework: overview of main relevant statutes/papers

RE-Act (*EEG*):

- Aiming at the protection of the climate and the environment, the security and sustainability of energy supply and the promotion of renewable energy sources;
- Priority principle (*Vorrangprinzip*);
- TSOs' duties (i.e. OWP operators' rights):
  a) Duty to connect (*Anschlusspflicht*),
  b) Duty to purchase, transmit and distribute (*Pflicht zur Abnahme, Übertragung und Verteilung*),
  c) Duty to remunerate/payment of feed-in tariff (*Vergütungspflicht*),
  d) Duty to expand grid capacity (*Netzerweiterungspflicht*),
  e) Other duties.
- Legal and investment security/protection of investors' confidence (*Vertrauensschutz*);
- One of the most successful feed-in laws in the world.

EI-Act (*EnWG*):

- TSOs' duties (i.e. OWP operators' rights):
  a) Duty to connect OWP to the onshore grid (*Netzanschlusspflicht*),
  b) Duty to cover OWP grid connection costs (*Kostenübernahme*)

GFNA (*BNetzA*) position paper:

- Project developers' duty to provide sufficient evidence that OWP will materialise (*Realisierungsnachweis*);
- Definition of criteria for grid connection (*Anbindungskriterien*) to improve legal, planning and investment security of OWP project developers;
- TSOs' duties (i.e. OWP operators' rights):
  a) Duty to issue conditional grid connection undertaking (*bedingte Netzanbindungszusage*) and to connect OWP to the grid within 30 months after the issuance of such undertaking,
  b) Duty to issue unconditional grid connection undertaking (*unbedingte Netzanbindungszusage*).

Figure 5: Legal framework - overview of main relevant statutes/papers

After having discussed the RE-Act (*EEG*) and the EI-Act (*EnWG*) in the course of this section which are the two main legal statutes most relevant for OWP investors in Germany and which stipulate clear and far reaching rights for OWP operators (see Figure 5), the subsequent section now deals in detail with the approval process which is necessary to realise an OWP project in the German EEZ.

4.2 Getting approval for the construction of an OWP

As previously mentioned, the erection of an OWP in Germany is subject to the approval of the relevant authorities. When planning the construction of an OWP, project developers should be aware of the fact that such an approval cannot be granted over night. Even if the necessary approval process for an OWP in the German EEZ runs very smoothly, it typically takes about 2 years. Hence, a well-prepared OWP project developer should be familiar with the relevant applicable legal regimes regulating the approval process and have good knowledge about the approval process

---

90 The much more important question is rather what kind of events are to be considered force majeure and what kind of events not. There is no doubt that the weather risk is normally defined as a force majeure event. However, whether delayed supplies to the TSO should also qualify as a force majeure event is another story. This may be rather a question of agreeing proper liquidated damages in the respective supply contracts.

itself to avoid unnecessary failures (e.g. incomplete or insufficient OWP project application documents), which normally go along with a delayed approval of the OWP project at significant additional costs for the OWP developer, or which could theoretically even result in a rejection of the project[91]. In a nutshell, OWP developers should try to reduce the probability that an approval is not granted as much as possible.

The legal basis for that approval to be granted and the main relevant legal statutes applicable are discussed in *Section 4.2.1.*

The subsequent *Section 4.2.2* deals with the approval procedure for OWP in the German EEZ itself and the individual approval phases an applicant has to go trough.[92]

4.2.1 Legal basis and main applicable statutes

The approval process for OWP in the German EEZ in general is based on the Marine Facilities Ordinance, MFO (*Seeanlagenverordnung, SeeAnlV*), which specifically regulates the necessary individual steps and requirements to be considered by the FMHA (*BSH*). A good knowledge of such legal statute is important for an OWP developer to be well prepared when approaching the FMHA (*BSH*) with his application documents. The provisions most relevant will be discussed in the following *Section 4.2.1.1.*

Furthermore, the FMHA (*BSH*) has developed spatial plans (*Raumordnungspläne*) for the German EEZ[93] on the basis of the Federal Spatial Planning Act, FSPA (*Raumordnungsgesetz, ROG*) to help better coordinate the recovery of the sea which is exposed to various and often conflicting marine uses, but in particular to accelerate the

91 Considering the fact that available offshore wind energy priority areas in the German EEZ are limited and thus it is not rare that the applications of different OWP projects compete for the same offshore site (see Appendix D, question 3), good knowledge about the FMHA (*BSH*) approval process can be a key advantage.

92 The vast majority of OWP to be installed in Germany will be located in the German EEZ, and only a very small number of OWP do or will operate in the German Territorial Sea. Hence, this section focuses solely on the approval process required by law for the construction of OWP in the German EEZ to allow for a more detailed analysis of the subject matter. Furthermore, available areas in the German Territorial Sea for installing (large) OWP are very limited and are by far not sufficient to implement the German government's ambitious growth plans for offshore wind energy. Finally, compared to OWP erected in the German Territorial Sea, OWP located further out at sea in the German EEZ are much more accepted by the general public, as they are usually not visible from the coast. Thus, the natural scenery remains largely unaffected (see FMHA (*BSH*), Non-technical summary (North Sea): environmental report, undated, p. 23, http://www.bsh.de/en/Marine_uses/Spatial_Planning_in_the_ German _EEZ/index. jsp (accessed 20 June 2011)).

93 Spatial plans have been introduced for the German EEZ of the North and the Baltic Sea.

development of the German offshore wind energy industry in such areas. The introduction of those spatial plans had of course a direct impact on the approval process for OWP to be erected in the German EEZ as the FMHA (*BSH*) has to consider the guidelines of that spatial planning when reviewing a new OWP project (see *Section 4.2.1.2*).

4.2.1.1 Marine Facilities Ordinance

The MFO (*SeeAnlV*) is based on the United Nations Convention on the Law of the Sea, UNCLOS (*Seerechtsübereinkommen der Vereinten Nationen, SRÜ*)[94] and the Federal Maritime Responsibilities Act, FMRA (*Seeaufgabengesetz, SeeAufgG*),[95] and governs the whole approval process for OWP in the German EEZ.[96]

Before an operator or investor can start with the construction of an OWP, he has to apply for an approval by the FMHA (*BSH*)[97], which verifies whether any grounds for a rejection do exist or not. The reasons which could lead to a refusal of such an application are as follows: a potential negative impact on the safety or efficiency of the maritime traffic, and/or negative effects on the marine environment, or a conflict with the spatial planning for the German EEZ.[98]

94 The sovereignty of a coastal state (*Küstenstaat*) ends at the 12-Mile Zone and thus does not extend to the EEZ sea belt further out at the sea. The latter area is instead subject to a special legal regime (*besondere Rechtsordnung*), which assigns to the respective coastal state sovereign rights (*souveräne Rechte*) and specific jurisdiction (*Hoheitsbefugnisse*), regarding, e.g. the production of energy from wind and the exclusive right to construct, authorise and regulate the construction of facilities in the EEZ (see Part II, Section 1, Article 2 and Part V, Article 55-60 UNCLOS (*SRÜ*); for an in-depth analysis on the application of UNCLOS (*SRÜ*) in the EEZ please refer to Maier, Die Ausdehnung des Raumordnungsgesetzes auf die Ausschließliche Wirtschaftszone (AWZ) dargestellt an der auslösenden Situation der raumordnerischen Steuerung von Offshore-Windenergieanlagen, 2008, pp. 62 et seq.). The aforementioned legal provisions include also the right to approve the construction of OWP (see Klinski, Rechtliche Probleme der Zulassung von Windkraftanlagen in der ausschließlichen Wirtschaftszone (AWZ), 2001, p. 10).

95 The FMRA (*SeeAufgG*) assigns the authorization to examine and approve facilities (including OWP) in the German EEZ to the German federal state (*Bund*), who in turn has assigned this right to the FMHA (*BSH*) (see Section 1, No. 10a and Section 5 (1), No. 4 FMRA (*SeeAufgG*)).

96 See Article 1.1, No. 1 and 1.2, No. 1 MFO (*SeeAnlV*). On the contrary, the approval process of OWP within the Territorial Sea (i.e. 12-Mile Zone) is governed by the laws and regulations of the respective federal coastal state (*Küstenbundesland*) (see FMHA (*BSH*) http://www.bsh.de/en/Marine_uses/Industry/Wind_farms/index.jsp (accessed 22 June 2011).

97 See Article 2 MFO (*SeeAnlV*). The German legislator prohibits the construction of OWP in the EEZ as long as no approval has been granted for such kind of projects by the FMHA (*BSH*), a higher federal authority in Germany belonging to the Federal Ministry of Transport, Building and Urban Development *(Bundesministerium für Verkehr, Bau und Stadtentwicklung*). In German legal literature such approach is often called a preventive ban subject to permit (*präventives Verbot mit Erlaubnisvorbehalt*) (see Klinski, Rechtliche Probleme der Zulassung von Windkraftanlagen in der ausschließlichen Wirtschaftszone (AWZ), 2001, p. 45). Nevertheless, the FMHA (*BSH*) has the right to exempt facilities not endangering the marine environment from the duty to apply for an approval according to Article 10 MFO (*SeeAnlV*).

98 Simplified description (for more details see Article 3 MFO (*SeeAnlV*)).

While examining a specific OWP project, the FMHA (*BSH*) shall consider opinions and statements of other public authorities in its decision making process whose administrative fields are affected by the project. These public authorities include, e.g., the Federal Research Institute for Fishery (*Bundesforschungsanstalt für Fischerei*), the Federal Environment Agency (*Umweltbundesamt*), and the respective State Mining Authority (*Landesbergamt*). However, consideration in this respect does not mean that those statements have a binding effect on the FMHA (*BSH*)' final decision, which remains independent in this regard.[99] Hence, the requirement in question can be rather interpreted as a duty to extend the basis of information and to analyse the project from different view points to ensure a well-educated final decision of the FMHA (*BSH*). In contrast to the public authorities mentioned above, the responsible regional Waterways and Shipping Directorate, WSD (*Wasser- und Schifffahrtsdirektion, WSD*),[100] and the Federal Agency for Nature Conservation, FANC (*Bundesamt für Naturschutz, BfN*),[101] must give its consent to the OWP project in any event before an approval can be finally granted by the FMHA (*BSH*).

Furthermore, usually an Environmental Impact Assessment, EIA (*Umweltverträglichkeitsprüfung, UVP*) has to be conducted by the OWP developer in the course of the approval process to enable a better evaluation of the probability and the magnitude of potential (negative) impacts on the marine environment.[102]

Besides the aforementioned requirement to conduct an EIA (*UVP*), the FMHA (*BSH*) must also consider European legislation on the protection of the (marine) environ-

---

99 See Article 5 (3) MFO (*SeeAnlV*) and Klinski, Rechtliche Probleme der Zulassung von Windkraftanlagen in der ausschließlichen Wirtschaftszone (AWZ), 2001, p. 68.

100 See Article 6 MFO (*SeeAnlV*) and FMHA (*BSH*), http://www.bsh.de/en/Marine_uses/ Industry/Wind_farms/Approval_Procedure.jsp (accessed 22 June 2011).

101 With its last revision in March 2010, the Federal Nature Conservation Act (*Bundesnaturschutzgesetz*) was extended to the German EEZ. Thus, in addition to the required FMHA (*BSH*) approval, a separate approval to be granted by the FANC (*BfN*) became necessary when planning the erection of an OWP in the German EEZ.

102 According to Article 2a MFO (*SeeAnlV*), an EIA (*UVP*) is obligatory for all OWP which are covered by the definition of Article 3 EIA-Act (*UVPG*) and, at the same time, do require an approval by the FMHA (*BSH*) according to Article 2 MFO (*SeeAnlV*). However, for OWP consisting of at least 20 windmill-powered plants with an overall size of each plant of more than 50 m, such EIA (*UVP*) has to be conducted in any case (see Article 3b (1) and Appendix 1, Clause 1.6.1 EIA-Act (*UVPG*)). OWP in the German EEZ do normally easily meet both requirements (in size and in number of plants), as they would be barely economically feasible otherwise due to the long distance to the coast. To achieve more transparency and further reduce uncertainties in the course of the OWP project's environmental assessment, the FMHA (*BSH*) has recently developed a predefined standard ("Standard: Investigation of the Impacts of Offshore Wind Turbines on the Marine Environment"), which has to be considered by the respective applicant when performing its EIA (*UVP*) (see FMHA (*BSH*) web page, http://www.bsh.de/en/Products/Books/ Standard/index.jsp (accessed 25 June 2011)).

ment applicable when examining a new OWP project in the German EEZ, e.g. the EU directives on the conservation of natural habitats and of wild fauna and flora (*FFH-Richtlinie*)[103] and on the conservation of wild birds (*Vogelschutzrichtlinie*).[104] The (marine) areas protected under these legal regimes do belong to an European ecological network of special areas of conservation and protection called "Natura 2000",[105] and the FMHA (*BSH*) must take into account the provisions of those EU directives in its decision making process as far as a protected "Natura 2000" area is concerned.[106] However, we will learn in the subsequent *Section 4.2.1.2* that the German legislator has established an even stricter approach when it comes to the potential construction of OWP in such "Natura 2000" areas.

In case there are no concerns foreseeable regarding the aforementioned environmental matters or when one can validly assume that (potential) minor negative effects caused by the construction and operation of an OWP can be successfully remedied or compensated, the applicant has the right to get approval from the FMHA (*BSH*) for his project.[107] The permit granted can be transferred (*übertragen*) to an alternative operator or investor. However, the transfer must be announced to the FMHA (*BSH*).[108]

Furthermore, the FMHA (*BSH*) has the possibility to grant its approval subject to the fulfilment of specific project-related conditions and will make use of it if it deems necessary for a certain project. In addition, every FMHA (*BSH*) approval typically

---

103 Council Directive 92/43/EEC

104 Council Directive 79/409/EEC. See also Klinski, Rechtliche Probleme der Zulassung von Windkraftanlagen in der ausschließlichen Wirtschaftszone (AWZ), 2001, p. 25.

105 For further information see EU web page, http://europa.eu/rapid/pressReleasesAction.do?reference=MEMO/05/294&format=HTML&aged=0&language=EN&guiLanguage=en (accessed 25 June 2011).

106 For an overall summary of applicable international, European and national legislation on the protection of the environment in Germany please refer to FMHA (*BSH*), Umweltbericht zum Raumordnungsplan für die deutsche ausschließliche Wirtschaftszone (AWZ) in der Nordsee, pp. 17-21, http://www.bsh.de/de/ Meeresnutzung/Raumordnung_in_der_AWZ/index.jsp (accessed 25 June 2011).

107 In this case, the FMHA (*BSH*) has no administrative discretion (*kein Ermessensspielraum*) and is bound to grant its approval (*gebundene Entscheidung*). However, the approval granted does not have a so-called concentration effect (*keine Konzentrationswirkung*) (see Maier, Die Ausdehnung des Raumordnungsgesetzes auf die Ausschließliche Wirtschaftszone (AWZ) dargestellt an der auslösenden Situation der raumordnerischen Steuerung von Offshore-Windenergieanlagen, 2008, p. 26, and Klinski, Rechtliche Probleme der Zulassung von Windkraftanlagen in der ausschließlichen Wirtschaftszone (AWZ), 2001, p. 15). At the moment, the necessary FANC (*BfN*) approval must be still obtained separately, but this might be soon no longer necessary. However, as of to date, the separate approvals to be granted by the responsible WSD and the respective TSO (for grid connection) will remain.

108 For further details see Article 14 (5) MFO (*SeeAnlV*) and Wustlich, Das Recht der Windenergie im Wandel - Teil 2: Windenergie auf See, 2007, pp. 128-129.

contains rather standard conditions which apply to all approved OWP, such as setting time limits for the commencement of the OWP construction to avoid unreasonable delays[109], asking for compliance with specific and/or generally recognised technological standards[110], setting limits for noise emissions (*Lärmemissionen*), as well as requiring the removal of the OWP facilities once the approval/license granted has expired (usually after 25 years)[111]. If the OWP operator should not comply with one or more of the conditions outlined above, the FMHA (*BSH*) has the right to revoke its approval.

The approval granted by the FMHA (*BSH*) must be published by public announcement. If no objections have been submitted by an opposing party within one month after the announcement, the approval is valid and an appeal (*Widerspruch*) against it is no longer possible, which gives an OWP project developer a high degree of legal certainty (protection of confidence (*Vertrauensschutz*)).[112]

Even though one can assume that prospects of success are rather less promising, it shall be nevertheless mentioned that the applicant has the right to file an action (*Klageeinreichung*)[113], if the FMHA (*BSH*) should grant an approval subject to a

---

109 In the past, the standard time limit within which the construction of an OWP had to be started was 2 years after its approval. Today, this time limit is variable and is determined by the FMHA (*BSH*) on a case-by-case basis depending on the specifics of the individual project (see Appendix D, question 5).

110 See Article 4 (1), (4), Article 5 (2) MFO (*SeeAnlV*). The OWP operator is required to use state-of-the-art technology (*Stand der Technik*). In addition to the STEA (*StUK*) to be considered when performing the EIA (*UVP*) (see footnote 102), the project developer must also comply with the "Standard: Ground Investigations for Offshore Wind Farms (*Standard: Baugrunderkennung für Offshore-Windenergieparks*)" and the "Standard: Design of Offshore Wind Turbines (*Standard: Konstruktive Ausführung von Offshore-Windenergieanlagen*)". The latter contains binding technical requirements for each of the following specific OWP project phases: development and design, construction and implementation, operation, deconstruction (see FMHA (*BSH*) web page, http://www.bsh.de/en/Products/Books/Standard/index.jsp).

111 See Article 12 (1) MFO (SeeAnlV) and FMHA (*BSH*), http://www.bsh.de/en/Marine_ uses/Industry/Wind_farms/Approval_Procedure.jsp (accessed 22 June 2011). To ensure an orderly removal of the OWP facilities by the OWP operator, the FMHA (*BSH*) has the right to require adequate security from the applicant if it deems it necessary (see Article 12 (3) and Appendix MFO (SeeAnlV)). The FMHA (*BSH*) normally makes use of this right. Typically, a corporate or bank guarantee will be required covering the expected costs of such removal. As a rule of thumb, Mr. Dahlke states that the expected costs of removal will be slightly less than the installation costs of the OWP (see Appendix D, question 7). KMPG calculates removal costs of about EUR 0.2 mn/MW (see KPMG, Offshore Windparks in Europa - Marktstudie 2010, 2010, p. 82).

112 Once the period has expired, an approval can only be revoked (*Widerruf*) by the FMHA (*BSH*), if new findings or information arguing against the project have suddenly emerged, which were not available when the respective approval was granted. However, even in such cases it is rather likely that a subsequent revocation of a FMHA (*BSH*) approval would come along with the project developer's right to claim an indemnity for any damages suffered (see Appendix D, question 2).

113 See Klinski, Rechtliche Probleme der Zulassung von Windkraftanlagen in der ausschließlichen Wirtschaftszone (AWZ), 2001, p. 71.

condition to which the applicant cannot agree or should even completely reject the requested approval for building an OWP.

If the FMHA (*BSH*) should receive competing requests from independent applicants for the approval of the erection of an OWP in the same marine area, it shall give priority to the request which has fulfilled and provided all necessary information first and thus is ready for approval (*genehmigungsfähig*).[114]

Finally, the FMHA (*BSH*) has identified and established particularly suitable areas (*besondere Eignungsgebiete*) for OWP in the German EEZ to reduce uncertainties among potential OWP operators and/or investors and to accelerate a systematic construction of OWP in these identified special areas,[115] which have been later converted into wind energy priority areas (*Vorranggebiete*) in the course of the introduction of Germany's spatial planning for the German EEZ[116].

4.2.1.2 Spatial planning for the German EEZ

As discussed in Section 3.2, the German government is pursuing an intense growth strategy for the renewable energy sector due to the intended phase-out of nuclear energy in Germany until 2022, with offshore wind energy being the major driving force. OWP in the German EEZ shall contribute a considerable portion to the future energy mix of Germany. To achieve this goal, the German government has passed a multitude of legal provisions in the recent past to promote a fast construction and installation of OWP in that area. The introduction of the spatial planning for the German EEZ has been an important aspect as well.

Before the respective spatial plans for the German EEZ of the North and Baltic Seas were determined, potential OWP investors faced a lack of planning reliability and thus had difficulties to evaluate the probability of a successful realisation of OWP projects. This often led to a resistance to invest[117]. The main problems have been as

---

114 The so-called priority principle (*Prioritätsprinzip*) applies (see Article 5 (1) MFO (*SeeAnlV*) and Dannecker/Kerth, Die rechtlichen Rahmenbedingungen für Offshore-Windenergieanlagen in der deutschen Ausschließlichen Wirtschaftszone (AWZ), 2009, p. 751). Competing applications for the same sea site are not uncommon in practice as the amount of promising priority OWP areas is rather limited (see Appendix D, question 3), which is one more good argument for an OWP project developer to arrange for a fast and efficient approval process.

115 See Article 3a MFO (*SeeAnlV*).

116 See subsequent Section 4.2.1.2 for more details.

117 The definition of particularly suitable areas for OWP in the German EEZ according to Article 3a MFO (SeeAnlV) was a first step in the right direction to improve the environment for OWP investors (see also Section 4.2.1.1 above). This concept was finally replaced and refined by a more

follows: Firstly, a multitude of different marine uses (such as energy production, shipping, conservation areas and the sea(bed) as food and raw material source[118]) and the rising need for the coordination of growing conflicts between them and secondly, the legislator's impossibility to regulate and influence the developments in the German EEZ due to a missing legal basis for setting a sustainable and integrated spatial plan in this area. The reason for the latter was that the German Federal Spatial Planning Act, FSPA (*Raumordnungsgesetz, ROG*) was only applicable in the German national territory but not in the German EEZ at the time.

So, what did the German legislator do to arrange for both a proper coordination of all the individual marine uses in the German EEZ on the one hand, and the continuous promotion of the German offshore wind industry by further improving the (legal) environment to encourage OWP investors' confidence on the other hand?

Due to the continuous progress in the offshore wind energy sector and the increased number of planned OWP projects, it became inevitable to set up a framework for a sustainable development of the marine areas in the German EEZ. Therefore, the German legislator finally extended the legal provisions of the FSPA (*ROG*) to the German EEZ in 2004[119], thereby laying the foundation for the development of a sustainable spatial plan for such area and the minimization of future conflicts between opposing marine uses[120].

Besides being in charge of the overall approval process for individual OWP projects, the FMHA (*BSH*) in addition took over the responsibility for the development of the respective spatial plans for the German EEZ[121]. The bundling of those interrelated tasks within one competency assured the availability of the necessary specific know-

---

integrated approach with the introduction of the spatial planning for the German EEZ and the definition of wind energy priority areas.

118 See FMHA (*BSH*), Attachment - Spatial Plan for the EEZ in the North Sea, 2009, p. 3, http://www.bsh.de/en/Marine_uses/Spatial_Planning_in_the_German_EEZ/index.jsp (accessed 22 June 2011) and Maier, Die Ausdehnung des Raumordnungsgesetzes auf die Ausschließliche Wirtschaftszone (AWZ) dargestellt an der auslösenden Situation der raumordnerischen Steuerung von Offshore-Windenergieanlagen, 2008, p. 16.

119 See Section 1 (4) FSPA (*ROG*). The implementation of such an extension clause (*Erstreckungsklausel*) in the German FSPA (*ROG*) is valid and does not contradict with the legal provisions of the UNCLOS (*SRÜ*) (for further information see Maier, Die Ausdehnung des Raumordnungsgesetzes auf die Ausschließliche Wirtschaftszone (AWZ) dargestellt an der auslösenden Situation der raumordnerischen Steuerung von Offshore-Windenergieanlagen, 2008, pp. 11, 50 and 63 et seq.).

120 See Section 1 (1) and (2) and Section 3 (1) No. 2 FSPA (*ROG*).

121 See Section 17 (3) FSPA (*ROG*).

how, an adequate consideration and effective processing of new information and findings, as well as an efficient overall OWP approval process.

Nevertheless, it took the FMHA (*BSH*) about five years from the extension of the FSPA (*ROG*) to introduce its spatial plans for the German EEZ of both the North and the Baltic Sea.[122] The promotion of offshore wind energy and a speedy development of its full potential are two of the main guidelines (*Leitlinien*) on the basis of which these plans have been developed.[123] That is why the FMHA (*BSH*) has made use of its right to define so-called wind energy priority areas (*Vorranggebiete*) for the erection of OWP.[124] Those areas have been identified under the assumption of a full utilization (*vollständige Bebauung*) by OWP still to be erected, and the FMHA (*BSH*) came to the conclusion that no significant negative effects on the marine environment have to be expected in these areas when considering that kind of scenario. This is also the case for the seascape (*Meerespanorama*), as the defined wind energy priority areas are far out at sea (> 30 km).[125]

With the establishment of the respective spatial plans for the German EEZ in accordance with the FSPA (*ROG*), three particularly suitable areas (*besondere Eignungsgebiete*), previously defined in accordance with the provisions of the MFO (*SeeAnlV*), have been transformed into wind energy priority areas (North Sea: "Nördlich Borkum"; Baltic Sea: "Kriegers Flak" and "Westlich Adlergrund"). In addition, two

122 The spatial plans for the German EEZ of the North and Baltic Sea entered into force on 26 September 2009 and 19 December 2009 respectively (see Appendix J, K and FMHA (*BSH*), http://www.bsh.de/en/Marine_uses/Spatial_Planning_in_the_German_ EEZ/index.jsp (accessed 22 June 2011)). Before the introduction of a spatial plan, the FMHA (*BSH*) had to conduct an EIA (*UVP*) by itself, announce the spatial plan to the general public, and involve other public authorities whose administrative fields might be affected (see Section 9 (1), 10 (1) and 15 (3) FSPA (*ROG*)). However, the forward-looking EIA (*UVP*) to be made by the FMHA (*BSH*) in the course of the general spatial planning does not replace the OWP project-specific EIA (*UVP*) to be arranged for by the operator in the course of the approval process at the FMHA (*BSH*) (see Article 2a MFO (*SeeAnlV*)).

123 For an overview of all guidelines considered please refer to FMHA (*BSH*), Attachment - Spatial Plan for the EEZ in the North Sea, 2009, p. 4, http://www.bsh.de/en/Marine_ uses/ Spatial_Planning_in_the_German_EEZ/ index.jsp (accessed 22 June 2011).

124 See Section 8 (7) No. 1 FSPA (*ROG*). Apart from the erection of wind turbines, the status of a wind energy priority area also includes the necessary ancillary facilities, such as converter and monitoring platforms as well as transformer stations. The laying of the undersea cable is covered too, for which the spatial plans regarding the German EEZ have even considered separate priority areas in addition (see FMHA (*BSH*), Anlagen zur Verordnung über die Raumordnung in der deutschen ausschließlichen Wirtschaftszone in der Nordsee, pp. 10 et seq., 18, http://www.bsh.de/de/ Meeresnutzung/Raumordnung_in_der_AWZ index.jsp (accessed 25 June 2011)).

125 See FMHA (*BSH*), Umweltbericht zum Raumordnungsplan für die deutsche ausschließliche Wirtschaftszone (AWZ) in der Nordsee, pp. 346, 357, 463,http:// www.bsh.de/de/Meeresnutzung/Raumordnung_in_der_AWZ/index.jsp (accessed 25 June 2011).

new wind energy priority areas have been introduced in the North Sea ("Östlich Austerngrund" and "Südlich Amrumbank")[126]. These areas are exclusively reserved for wind energy purposes (*Freihaltefunktion*), which means that any other alternative marine use is not allowed should it be in conflict with the potential construction of an OWP[127]. However, the erection of an OWP in the remaining part of the German EEZ is not prohibited (*keine Ausschlusswirkung*) and thus still possible if approved by the FMHA (*BSH*).[128] The only exclusion zone for wind energy purposes (*Ausschlussgebiet*), covering about 28% of the German EEZ, are the earmarked "Natura 2000" areas already referred to in the previous section. That means that the erection of OWP in such areas is completely prohibited in Germany, whereas existing EU legislation on the protection of the environment only requires the consideration of the applicable EU directives when examining the erection of an OWP in a Natura 2000 area.[129]

Lots of additional OWP have to be erected to meet the ambitious targets of the German government. Due to the limited size of available wind energy priority areas in the German EEZ[130], the spatial plans require that the installation of the individual

---

126 The maps attached in Appendix J and K show the positions of the existing wind energy priority areas in the German EEZ.

127 The identified wind energy priority areas have the effect of an anticipated supporting expert opinion (*antizipiertes unterstützendes Sachverständigengutachten*) in the course of an OWP approval process, i.e. this opinion is a positive indicator, but with no binding effect on the FMHA (*BSH*) to finally approve the project. However, the FMHA (*BSH*) can actually only deny approval in cases where project-specific matters are problematic or if new relevant general technical or environmental information has to be considered by it, which was not available when the wind energy priority area concerned was defined (see Appendix D, question 9). So, in practice a rejection by the FMHA (*BSH*) to grant approval for an OWP to be erected in a previously defined wind energy priority area is rather unlikely if the individual project determinants are sound. However, project developers should note that OWP to be erected in such wind energy priority areas must nevertheless comply with the respective environmental requirements considered in Article 2a and 3 MFO (SeeAnlV) and Article 38 FNCA (*BNatSchG*), i.e. the duties to conduct an EIA (*UVP*) and to consider relevant species and biotope protection regulation. For a detailed analysis of the legal effects of such expert opinion please refer to Maier, Die Ausdehnung des Raumordnungsgesetzes auf die Ausschließliche Wirtschaftszone (AWZ) dargestellt an der auslösenden Situation der raumordnerischen Steuerung von Offshore-Windenergieanlagen, 2008, pp. 32-36.

128 See Wustlich, Das Recht der Windenergie im Wandel - Teil 2: Windenergie auf See, 2007, p. 123, and Frenz/Müggenborg, Erneuerbare-Energien-Gesetz Kommentar, 2010, p. 667.

129 However, OWP projects which have been approved already in Natura 2000 areas before the introduction of the spatial plans for the German EEZ, as well as projects which have been already in an advanced stage for approval at the time have been exempted by the legislator (protection of investor's confidence (*Vertrauensschutz*)).

130 The overall size of the current wind energy priority areas in the German EEZ amounts to 1,010 square km (North Sea: 880 square km; Baltic Sea: 130 square km; see also Appendix H and I). However, these priority areas are by now fully occupied by OWP already operating or by OWP projects approved or currently under review by the FMHA (*BSH*), which has received in the meantime even the first OWP applications for marine sites located outside the existing priority areas. According to the offshore wind industry a maximum capacity of 10,000 to 15,000 MW can be generated on the basis of the existing wind energy priority areas. Hence, the constitution of further priority areas is necessary for achieving the German government's ambitious aim of an

wind turbines in an OWP shall be as economical as possible (*flächensparend*), in order to ensure a maximum efficiency of the use of the respective areas (i.e. to safe space and keep potential negative environmental impacts at a minimum).[131]

Within this and the previous section the legal basis for the approval process of OWP in the German EEZ has been discussed. The MFO (*SeeAnlV*) sets a transparent framework to be considered by the FMHA (*BSH*) and OWP project developers in the course of the conduction of the necessary OWP approval process. Furthermore, the introduction of the spatial plans for the German EEZ in the North and Baltic Sea has clearly reduced conflicts between the different marine uses.

Figure 6: OWP approval process - legal basis and main applicable statutes

Moreover, the legislator's spatial planning even considers priority areas for wind energy purposes to further accelerate the construction of OWP in the German EEZ (see Figure 6), which led to a considerable improvement of the planning reliability for potential OWP investors as well as to a much faster and more efficient processing of the OWP approval process by the FMHA (*BSH*). The individual phases of the FMHA (*BSH*) approval process are described and discussed in the following section.

available offshore electricity production level of 25,000 MW in 2030. According to Mr. Dahlke it is very likely that new wind energy priority areas will be determined in the course of 2012 (see Appendix D, question 10, and FMHA (*BSH*), Anlagen zur Verordnung über die Raumordnung in der deutschen ausschließlichen Wirtschaftszone in der Nordsee (p. 19) bzw. Ostsee (p. 18), http://www.bsh.de/de/Meeresnutzung/ Raumordnung_in_der_AWZ/index.jsp (accessed 25 June 2011)).

131 See FMHA (*BSH*), Anlagen zur Verordnung über die Raumordnung in der deutschen ausschließlichen Wirtschaftszone in der Nordsee (pp. 17 et seq.) bzw. Ostsee (pp. 15 et seq.), http://www.bsh.de/de/Meeresnutzung/Raumordnung_in_der_AWZ/ index.jsp (accessed 25 June 2011)

4.2.2 Phases of the OWP approval process

The previous sections of chapter 4.2 provided an insight into the legal statutes which have to be considered by the FMHA (*BSH*) when examining the application for a new OWP project. As indicated above, a basic understanding of the legal provisions concerned is beneficial for an OWP project developer when planning to realise an OWP in Germany. However, it is at least of the same importance for a potential OWP investor or project developer to have sound knowledge about the overall OWP approval process itself, and about the specific contributions and requirements he personally has to comply with in the course of the individual approval phases to avoid a delayed approval and additional costs.

A project developer's application for an OWP should contain detailed information about all relevant aspects, such as:

a) a precise description of the overall OWP project itself and the marine area where the project shall be installed including the reasoning why the specific area has been chosen;

b) a convincing technical conception, e.g. the selected type of wind turbine and a suitable foundation technique, a workable remote supervision concept (*Fernüberwachung*) and an evaluation of the possibilities for grid connection[132];

c) a first provisional assessment of the project's environmental impacts; and

d) an indicative timeline of the different phases of the project life cycle, i.e. preparation, construction, operation and deconstruction phase.[133]

Once the application has been submitted, the FMHA (*BSH*) will conduct a multi-stage OWP approval process (*mehrstufiger Genehmigungsprozess*) consisting of three consecutive approval phases or participations rounds (*Partizipationsrunden*), which are described in the following in more detail.

In the *first phase*, the FMHA (*BSH*) verifies whether all necessary aspects are covered in the application documents submitted and whether this information is sufficient to

---

[132] To further reduce uncertainties of the applicant, the FMHA (*BSH*) has developed certain technical standards (STEA (*STUK*)), which consider binding minimum requirements the applicant has to comply with when planning and erecting an OWP (see FMHA (*BSH*) web page, http://www.bsh.de/en/Products/Books/Standard/index.jsp (accessed 23 July 2011) and footnote 110).

[133] See Zeiler/Dahlke/Nolte, promet 2005, volume 31, No. 1, pp. 71-72.

make an educated decision about the OWP project introduced. If this is not the case, the applicant has the possibility to amend its application and to provide additional information where necessary. Although, the applicant's right to revise its documents is very important, one has to consider that every revision costs time. Thus, it is advisable for the project developer to maximize the quality and completeness of the first set of documents before submitting it to the competent authority to avoid any unnecessary delays.

At the same time, the FMHA (*BSH*) transfers the application documents received also to other related public authorities whose administrative fields are affected by the respective OWP project (e.g. regional WSD, State Mining Authority (*Landesbergamt*), FANC (*BfN*), FEA (*UBA*) and others), and asks them for comments (first participation round).[134] Overall, the first approval phase usually takes about 2 to 3 months.[135] However, a wise applicant should consider a certain buffer to have some time left to adjust his application in case the authorities involved identify a need for further amendments before entering the second phase as a revision of the application usually takes 2 to 6 months, depending on the extent of changes necessary.[136]

During the *second phase*, the FMHA (*BSH*) forwards the updated application documents once again to the authorities which have been involved in the first phase of review. Furthermore, additional parties, such as associations (*Verbände*) concerned (representing, inter alia, the interests of the wind energy industry itself, but also nature protection activist, and the shipping and fishery sector), the respective coastal state (*Küstenbundesland*) responsible for the approval of the OWP grid connection, and the general public[137] are invited to comment on the projected OWP at this approval stage. In case of any cross-border aspects applicable, even the competent authorities of the corresponding neighbouring state (*Nachbarstaat*) are involved

---

134 See FMHA (*BSH*) web page, http://www.bsh.de/en/Marine_uses/Industry/Wind_farms/ Approval_Procedure.jsp (accessed 23 July 2011).

135 According to the FMHA (*BSH*) the first approval phase usually only takes place if the respective OWP shall be erected in an unexplored marine area, i.e. a sea site where no OWP has been built or approved already before (non-availability of previous environmental studies or other relevant information/experiences), whereas, if such information is available, project developers can decide to omit the first approval phase and start directly with the second phase further described below (see Appendix D, question 6).

136 See Dahlke, Verfahren nach SeeAnlV, p. 2, http://www.erneuerbare-energien.de /files/pdfs/allgemein/application/pdf/dahlke_6.pdf (accessed 23 July 2011).

137 The projects are to be announced in nationwide daily newspapers, including the information that the respective application documents can be inspected at the premises of the FMHA (*BSH*) in Hamburg and Rostock (see Zeiler/Dahlke/Nolte, promet 2005, volume 31, No. 1, pp. 71-72).

(second participation round). Finally, an application conference takes place where the OWP developer or investor has the opportunity to present his project and where the scope of environmental investigations to be conducted is determined. The whole procedure of the second phase usually takes about 8 to 9 months.

Subsequently, the applicant has to arrange for an EIA (*UVP*)[138] covering the determined investigations and for a risk analysis of the probability of vessels colliding with the respective OWP installations, which usually takes up another 9 to 16 months. The indicative costs for such studies are borne by the investor and amount to EUR 1.0 to 1.5 mn. Before entering the third approval phase, the application documents are usually adjusted once more to consider the outcome and results of the environmental studies conducted.[139]

In the *third phase*, all parties which have been involved in the previous approval phases have the possibility to inspect the updated documents again as well as the results of the environmental studies conducted (third participation round). Subsequently, a discussion hearing (*Erörterungstermin*) takes place to reconsider whether further adjustment and/or improvement of the project documents is needed. Once, the documents are finalised, the FMHA (*BSH*) will commence with its final decision process and elaborate whether any reasons for denying approval (*Versagungsgründe*) of the OWP exist[140] or whether any environmental compensating measures (*Ausgleichs- und/oder Ersatzmaßnahmen*) are required[141]. If the respective OWP project is in line with the MFO (*SeeAnlV*) requirements, the FMHA (*BSH*) will and has to grant approval for it[142], which usually comes along with additional standard conditions as

---

138 This study usually contains a description of the status quo and an outlook of the potential impacts of the planned OWP project (*Bestandsbeschreibung und Auswirkungsprognose*) on the marine environment (e.g. ground, water, land- and seascape, human beings, fishes, birds) (see Zeiler/Dahlke/Nolte, promet 2005, volume 31, No. 1, pp. 71-73).

139 See FMHA (*BSH*) web page, http://www.bsh.de/en/Marine_uses/Industry/Wind_farms/ Approval_Procedure.jsp (accessed 23 July 2011), and Dahlke, Verfahren nach SeeAnlV, p. 2, http://www.erneuerbare-energien.de/files/pdfs/allgemein/application/ pdf/dahlke_6.pdf (accessed 23 July 2011).

140 The reasons to deny approval are listed in Article 3 MFO (SeeAnlV) and mentioned in Section 4.2.1.1 above.

141 If minor negative effects on the environment cannot be avoided even by the use of state-of-the-art technology, the FMHA (*BSH*) has the right to impose conditions to the investor to compensate for them (only if concrete compensation measures are not realizable for some reason the investor can also arrange for compensatory allowance (*Ersatzgeld*) (for further information see "Leitsätze für die Anwendung der Eingriffsregelung in der AWZ" available at: http:// www.bsh.de/de/Meeresnutzung/ Wirtschaft/Windparks/Gverfahren.jsp (accessed 23 July 2011)).

142 The burden of proof (*Beweislast*) of any reason to deny approval (*Versagensgründe*) lies with the FMHA (*BSH*), which is a very accommodating approach for potential OWP investors. In fact that means, that in cases of lack of knowledge/information about certain aspects, the FMHA (*BSH*) is

mentioned in the previous section. However, before the approval is finally communicated to the project developer, the regional WSD must confirm that the safety and efficiency of the maritime traffic is not negatively affected. Furthermore, on the basis of the results of the EIA (*UVP*), the FANC (*BfN*) must come to the conclusion that no negative impacts on the marine environment (protection of species and biotopes) have to be expected by the erection of the OWP project or, if so, clarify the question whether an exceptional approval can nevertheless be granted. Once these consents are available, the general public will be informed about such approval by newspaper announcement. Moreover, one has the possibility to inspect the approval documents at the FMHA (*BSH*) premises for one month. Overall, the final third approval phase takes about 4 to 6 months.[143]

Hence, a project developer should consider in its planning an overall approval process for an OWP of about 2.0 to 2.5 years, depending on whether relevant information about the respective marine area concerned is already available at the FMHA (*BSH*) or not (see Figure 7).

OWP approval process (approx. 2.0-2.5 years):			
First phase (2-3 months): - Review of application documents by FMHA (*BSH*); - Obtaining comments from related public authorities (first participation round); - Revision of application in case of need (might further extend first phase).	**Second phase (6-9 months):** - Obtaining comments from additional parties, such as concerned associations, the respective coastal state, public (second participation round); - Project presentation by developer/investor (application conference).	**Environmental impact assessment (9-16 months):** - Analysis of implications on marine environment and marine traffic; - Update of application documents.	**Third phase (4-6 months):** - Inspection of updated application documents by all involved parties (third participation round); - Discussion hearing; - Affirmative statements from the regional WSD and FANC (*BfN*); - Issuance of final approval by FMHA (*BSH*) and public disclosure.

Figure 7: Overview of phases of the OWP approval process

If the application requires major amendments or is incomplete, one might easily end up at the upper end of that range or would have to face an even longer approval process. Nevertheless, the multi-stage approval process outlined above is universally accepted in practice as it involves all relevant parties (including the respective coastal state in charge for the separate approval needed for the grid connection of the project)

nevertheless required to grant approval, as no proof/evidence for a potential negative effect can be given (see Maier, Die Ausdehnung des Raumordnungsgesetzes auf die Ausschließliche Wirtschaftszone (AWZ) dargestellt an der auslösenden Situation der raumordnerischen Steuerung von Offshore-Windenergieanlagen, 2008, pp. 30-31).

143 Today, the FMHA (*BSH*) is able to grant its approval much faster due to a higher degree of standardization, which led to a significant shortening of the final third approval phase compared to the situation some years ago (for further information see FMHA (*BSH*) web page, http://www.bsh.de/de/Meeresnutzung/Wirtschaft/ Windparks/Gverfahren.jsp (accessed 23 July 2011), Zeiler/Dahlke/Nolte, promet 2005, volume 31, No. 1, pp. 71-72, Dahlke, Verfahren nach SeeAnlV, p. 3, http://www.erneuerbare-energien.de/files/pdfs/allgemein/application/pdf/dahlke_6.pdf (accessed 23 July 2011) and Appendix D, question 6).

at a very early stage.[144] Thus, OWP project developers or investors have access to preliminary statements and positions of all important competent authorities and associations as well as the general public before they have to make their first considerable investment with regard to the OWP' approval process (i.e. the performance of an EIA (*UVP*)). However, based on the extensive information available at this stage, one should have sufficient planning reliability and investment security to predict the future prospects of his project as well as any potential risks attached to it (e.g. probability of rejection of approval).

4.3 Outlook

Even though the German government has made major efforts in the past to accelerate the development of the offshore wind energy industry and the erection of OWP in the German EEZ in particular, the current installed offshore wind energy capacity in Germany is rather disappointing and much lower than initially expected. For several reasons only a few OWP are in operation today despite a long project pipeline. Hence, German wind energy associations have formulated specific measures, which could further improve the environment for the realisation of OWP. The main cornerstones of such measures identified are mentioned in the following[145]:

a) Continuity of the statutory framework conditions of the RE-Act (*EEG*) and preservation of the priority principle for renewable energies[146] to maintain planning reliability for OWP investors;

b) Integration of the increased initial tariff (*erhöhte Anfangsvergütung* or *"Sprinterprämie"*) with regard to offshore wind energy into the initial tariff and thus removal of the 01 January 2016 deadline for commissioning considered so far in the RE-Act (*EEG*) [147];

---

144 See Dahlke, Verfahren nach SeeAnlV, p. 3, http://www.erneuerbare-energien.de/files/pdfs/allgemein/application/pdf/dahlke_6.pdf (accessed 23 July 2011).

145 See BWE, Positionspapier des Bundesverbandes WindEnergie e.V. (BWE e.V.) zur Novelle des Erneuerbare-Energien-Gesetzes, 2010, pp. 6-7, 15, http://www.wind-energie.de/sites/default/files/download/publication/bwe-positionspapier-zur-eeg-novelle-2012/bwe_position_eeg_novelle_20110107.pdf (accessed 11 September 2011), and Stiftung Offshore Windenergie et al., Positionspapier zur Offshore-Windenergie in Deutschland vom August 2010, 2010, pp. 2-3, http://www.eeg-aktuell.de/wp-content/ uploads/2010/07/Positionspapier-zur-Offshore-Windenergie-in-Deutschland-August-2010.pdf (accessed 09 September 2011).

146 Please refer to footnote 61 for further information.

147 Please refer to Section 4.1.1.2 for further information.

c) Deferral of applicable tariff/bonus reduction scheme (*Degression*) from 01 January 2015 to 01 January 2018[148];

d) Introduction of an optional compression model (*Stauchungsmodell*)[149];

e) General duty of the TSO to cover the costs caused by the connection of the OWP to the onshore grid[150]; and

f) Bundling of all approval competencies (*Genehmigungskompetenzen*) at the FMHA (*BSH*) to allow for a faster and more efficient OWP approval process and hereby more planning reliability for investors.

As discussed in Section 3.2 above, the German legislator's decision to accelerate the phase-out of nuclear energy has caused tremendous pressure to develop alternatives for energy supply very fast. According to the German government's energy plan, the renewable energy sector shall step in for the major part. With the governmental measures (*Maßnahmenpaket*) passed in June 2011 coming into effect as of 01 January 2012, the legislator has proven once more its flexibility and willingness to aid the renewable energy sector - and the field of offshore wind energy in particular - by the fast implementation of additional supportive measures.

When it comes to the realisation of OWP in the German EEZ, the relevant aspects or legal changes are the following[151]:

a) The statutory framework conditions of the RE-Act (*EEG*) as well as the priority principle for renewable energies remain in place to further facilitate investments (high degree of planning reliability);

---

148 Please refer to Section 4.1.1.2 for further information.

149 This compression model would go along with an increased initial tariff which is in return paid for a shorter period, which means that the scheme would come at no additional costs for the end customer. However, from a financing point of view, such option might be still advantageous, as banks might have more incentives to provide loans (faster repayment, shorter term loans, lower funding costs) and OWP investors receive their potential return on investment earlier (higher return on equity).

150 For further information see Section 4.1.2 and Article 17 (2a) in connection with 118 (3) El-Act (*EnWG*) in particular.

151 See Bundesregierung, Entwurf - Erfahrungsbericht 2011 zum Erneuerbare-Energien-Gesetz (EEG-Erfahrungsbericht), May 2011, pp. 118 et seq., http://www. bmu.de/files/pdfs/allgemein/application/pdf/eeg_erfahrungsbericht_2011_entwurf.pdf (accessed 11 September 2011), Bundesregierung, 10-Punkte-Sofortprogramm - Monitoring und Zwischenbericht der Bundesregierung, undated/b, pp. 1-2, http://www.bundesregierung.de/nsc_true/Content/DE/StatischeSeiten/Breg/Energie-konzept/Sofortprogramm,property=publicationFile.pdf/Sofortprogramm (accessed 11 September 2011) and Watson, Farley & Williams, Erneuerbare Energien in Deutschland - Briefing, 2011, pp. 1 et seq., http://www.wfw.com/Publications/ Publication891/$File/WFW%20-%20Renewable%20Energy%20in%20Germany% 202011%20-%20GERMAN.pdf (accessed 11 September 2011).

b) The increased initial tariff (*erhöhte Anfangsvergütung* or *"Sprinterprämie"*) with regard to offshore wind energy will be integrated into the initial tariff of the RE-Act (*EEG*), being then EUR 15.0 cents per kwh in total for the first 12 years[152];

c) The applicable tariff/bonus reduction scheme (*Degression*) will be deferred from 01 January 2015 to 01 January 2018, however, the applicable reduction rate for OWP increases from 5% to 7% per year[153];

d) Availability of an optional compression model (*Stauchungsmodell*) for OWP which reach commissioning (*Inbetriebnahme*) until 01 January 2018 (initial tariff of EUR 19.0 cents per kwh for the first 8 years), however, the normal initial tariff, according to point 2) above, will apply (i.e. EUR 15.0 cents per kwh) for any extended payment periods (depending on OWP' distance to coast and its water depth)[154];

e) Consideration of a general duty of TSO to cover the OWP grid connection costs (i.e. removal of currently applicable time limitation); and

f) The legislator intends to assign all authorities necessary for the approval of OWP in the German EEZ to the FMHA (*BSH*) to be more effective, to avoid unnecessary delays concerning the erection of OWP in the respective marine areas (e.g. reduction of reservation of offshore sites problem) and to provide additional planning reliability to investors (i.e. a separate FANC (*BfN*) approval would be no longer required)[155].

---

152 See Article 31 (2) draft RE-Act 2012 (*Entwurf EEG 2012*) (Bundesregierung, Gesetz für den Vorrang Erneuerbarer Energien (Erneuerbare-Energien-Gesetz - EEG), Konsolidierte (unverbindliche) Fassung des Gesetzestextes in der ab 1. Januar 2012 geltenden Fassung, undated/c, p. 30, http://www.bmu.de/files/pdfs/allgemein/ application/pdf/eeg_2012_bf.pdf (accessed 11 September 2011)).

153 See Article 20 (2) No. 7 a) draft RE-Act 2012 (*Entwurf EEG 2012*) (Bundesregierung, Gesetz für den Vorrang Erneuerbarer Energien (Erneuerbare-Energien-Gesetz - EEG), Konsolidierte (unverbindliche) Fassung des Gesetzestextes in der ab 1. Januar 2012 geltenden Fassung, undated/c, p. 30, http://www.bmu.de/files/pdfs/allgemein/ application/pdf/eeg_2012_bf.pdf (accessed 11 September 2011)).

154 See Article 31 (3) draft RE-Act 2012 (*Entwurf EEG 2012*) (Bundesregierung, Gesetz für den Vorrang Erneuerbarer Energien (Erneuerbare-Energien-Gesetz - EEG), Konsolidierte (unverbindliche) Fassung des Gesetzestextes in der ab 1. Januar 2012 geltenden Fassung, undated/c, p. 30, http://www.bmu.de/files/pdfs/allgemein/ application/pdf/eeg_2012_bf.pdf (accessed 11 September 2011)).

155 However, the regional WSD must still provide its consent to an OWP project before an FMHA (BSH) approval can be granted. The separate TSO' approval for the OWP' grid connection is still required too (see Appendix D, question 1).

In addition to the far-reaching improvements mentioned above, the legislator has also addressed one of the few remaining major obstacles for OWP project developers one could observe in the past:

From the beginning of 2012 onwards, the duration of the respective feed-in tariff payment (*Vergütungsdauer*) according to the RE-Act (*EEG*) shall be extended in cases of delayed grid connection and/or disturbances of the subsequent electricity transmission by the period of delay/disturbance suffered, even if the TSO has not acted negligently (i.e. also applicable in cases of act of god or force majeure risk)[156]. So far, such a risk had to be borne by the OWP project itself and has caused major concerns to OWP developers, sponsors and banks. Therefore, the new provision is a considerable step forward for the offshore wind industry, as it strongly improves the predictability of the OWP' cash flow (high planning reliability and investment security), which is of enormous advantage, especially when thinking about a non-recourse project finance structure.

Furthermore, the FMHA (*BSH*) intends to define additional wind energy priority areas in the Baltic Sea and the North Sea in 2012 to further push the continuous development and growth of the German offshore wind industry.[157]

To sum up, the governmental measures (*Maßnahmenpaket*) outlined above consider all major requirements of the offshore wind industry and even further far-reaching complementing measures. Moreover, the German legislator has passed and/or adjusted the necessary and relevant legal statutes very quickly and brings them into effect already at the beginning of 2012. Especially the introduction of the optional compression model, the assignment of all environment-related competent authorities to the FMHA (*BSH*) and the extension of the respective feed-in tariff payment period in cases of acts of god/force majeure are major improvements compared to the status quo. Thus, investors in OWP in the German EEZ can rely on a very accommodating investment environment with sufficient legal and planning reliability in the future.

---

156 See Section 4.1.2 and Article 31 (4) draft RE-Act 2012 (*Entwurf EEG 2012*) (Bundesregierung, Gesetz für den Vorrang Erneuerbarer Energien (Erneuerbare-Energien-Gesetz - EEG), Konsolidierte (unverbindliche) Fassung des Gesetzestextes in der ab 1. Januar 2012 geltenden Fassung, undated/c, pp. 30-31, http://www.bmu.de/ files/pdfs/allgemein/application/pdf/eeg_2012_bf.pdf (accessed 11 September 2011)).

157 See Appendix D, question 10.

4.4 Chapter summary

With the strengthening of the renewable energy sector in Germany it became obvious that the existing provisions of the relevant legal statutes, such as the RE-Act (*EEG*), the EI-Act (*EnWG*) or the MFO (*SeeAnlV*), were often not sufficient and sometimes even not clear enough to meet the challenges of the industry. Especially the German government's targeted strong growth of the offshore wind energy sector did not materialise for a long time due to various reasons. One of them was an insufficient legal set-up with obvious room for improvement. However, the German legislator was continuously determined to implement an efficient legal framework by adjusting existing and/or introducing new legal provisions where necessary to secure both the protection of the environment and the necessary legal and planning reliability to which potential OWP investors and project developers are looking for (e.g. by the consideration of a priority principle for renewable energies, improvement of offshore wind energy feed-in tariffs, requirement of TSO to cover OWP grid connection costs, definition of clarifying grid connection criteria, introduction of wind energy priority areas in the German EEZ, and the installation of an efficient and transparent OWP approval process).

Today, legal uncertainties have been reduced by the German legislator to a large extent. The legal adjustments outlined above have led to a significant improvement of the legal framework for the realisation of an OWP project. Overall, OWP investors nowadays can rely on a supporting political and legal environment in Germany providing for the investment security and planning reliability which is needed to realise complex OWP projects.

5. The bankability of OWP projects in Germany

In the previous two chapters, the political environment and the legal framework applicable when it comes to the realisation of an OWP project in the German EEZ have been reviewed and evaluated, as adequate policy support and legal certainty are with no doubt essential for a successful implementation of a sophisticated project like an OWP. However, it became obvious in the past that a solid and reliable political and legal framework alone is not sufficient to achieve the ambitious growth targets the legislator is pursuing for the German offshore wind industry. In fact, one could observe that the progress made with regard to the installed offshore wind energy capacity in Germany was much slower than initially expected. So, what was the reason for this shortfall and even more important what can be done to overcome it?

Experts agree that one of the major bottlenecks in the last years was the non-availability of sufficient debt financing to fund major projects like an OWP in the German EEZ. The impact of the financial crises, which led to a weakening of the whole banking industry and a subsequent growing risk sensitiveness of banks in general, is one of the main reasons why banks have been hesitant to finance such projects on a large scale in the past. However, the specifics of an OWP project in the German EEZ, for example the considerable technological challenges related to it, have increased the banks' resistance to finance such kind of projects even more. Especially the successful realisation of an OWP project structured as a (pure) project financing was therefore not possible until lately[158]. Hence, the first European OWP projects have been financed by plain corporate structures[159] mainly provided to major utilities, such as RWE AG or E.ON AG. However, to accomplish the targeted strong and fast growth of the offshore wind energy capacities in Germany, it is essential that the necessary funds can also be raised by a functional *project finance model*[160], as the expected total investment volume for OWP in the German EEZ with an amount of about EUR 30 bn and EUR 75 bn until 2020 and 2030 respectively cannot be provided solely by the corporate structures mainly used so far. Hence, next to a good knowledge of the applicable political and legal implications, it is also important for an OWP project developer to be aware of the opinions and main concerns of the banks active in the field of OWP financing. Which means in a nutshell to know: What makes an OWP project financing in the German EEZ bankable[161]?

Section 5.1 deals with the major challenges and bankability issues an OWP developer or investor should be aware of when thinking about raising funds for an OWP in Germany. The subsequent *Section 5.2* outlines typical market standards usually

---

158 The first real OWP project financing in Germany, Borkum West II, was closed in December 2010 and is currently under construction (see Appendix E, question 12).

159 For a description of the term "corporate structure" refer to Appendix C. The following remarks mainly focus on the existing challenges in connection with a successful implementation of a project finance structure for OWP in the German EEZ.

160 A definition of the term "project finance" can be found in Appendix A. Appendix B outlines the main project finance characteristics.

161 „Bankability is [...] the acceptability [...] of a project's structure as the basis of a project financing. [...] It is a very fluid concept, changing rapidly as market practice and sentiment change. It can also be a very deal-specific concept [...]." (see Vinter, Project Finance, 1998, p. 85).

considered by banks when providing financing for a German OWP and also briefly illustrates the possibilities to place such projects in the banking market. Finally, *Section 5.3* addresses some peculiarities when it comes to granting or taking collateral over an OWP in the German EEZ.

5.1 OWP (project) financing in Germany: major challenges and bankability issues

When planning an OWP project in the German EEZ, a good knowledge about the perception and the sensitivities of the banks which shall provide finance for the project is of great importance. The positions of the banks potentially involved should be considered by the project developer and sponsors rather sooner than later in the project development process. It might be even worthwhile to consult a bank/arranger with considerable offshore wind expertise already in a very early project stage to reduce the likelihood of a delayed project realisation and the potential need of a costly re-design of the project structure in an advanced development stage, or the risk to even set up a project structure which might be totally unacceptable for the banks.

So, sooner or later, the big question mark for every OWP project developer is: Is my OWP project bankable?

The main challenges coming along with the realisation of an OWP in the German EEZ from a bank's point of view, such as a reliable wind prognosis, related technology and grid connection risks and a convincing operation & maintenance concept, are outlined in the following. It will also be reviewed to what extent they could jeopardize a successful implementation of such a project and whether any measures are available to cure potential problems in practice.[162]

5.1.1 Wind prognosis

A precise prognosis of the wind conditions at the marine area where an OWP shall be erected is the central element of the project's earnings projections as the available supply of wind has direct influence on the cash flow generated by the project. Even small deviations in wind supply can have significant effects on the profitability of a project.[163] Hence, banks usually require two independent expert opinions on the

---

[162] Smart solutions to properly deal with those identified challenges become especially relevant when thinking about the use of a project finance structure to secure the funds needed.

[163] A doubling/bisection of wind speed increases/decreases the wind electricity generated by an OWG by the factor eight. Wind speeds suitable for electricity generation range between 4 m/s and

applicable wind conditions (*Windgutachten*) to evaluate the future prospects of an OWP project.[164] In addition, risk deductions (*Risikoabschläge*) on the forecasted wind supply are usually considered for certain standard and specific risks related to an OWP project.[165]

Naturally, the applicable wind conditions will always be a key risk driver of an OWP project. However, banks consider the related risk as manageable (*kontrollierbar*) and feel more and more comfortable with the available wind data (projections).[166]

5.1.2 Technology

The German offshore wind industry, being still in an early development stage, faces significant technological challenges which are much more demanding compared to the well-developed onshore wind sector. OWG are exposed to enormous physical loads and pressures due to a much harsher environment (higher wind speeds, heavy waves up to 25 m, salty and humid air which leads to corrosion and high temperature variations).[167]

Compared to other European countries involved in the offshore wind energy sector, the specifics of the German offshore wind market add even further complexity and difficulties. OWP projects in the German EEZ are usually located far out at sea (30 to 100 km) and face water depths up to 40 m. In addition, hub heights currently

---

25 m/s. Offshore wind speeds are usually more continuous and higher than onshore (offshore wind speed average: 9.5 m/s) (see IEA, World Energy Outlook 2010, 2010, p. 300, Böttcher, Finanzierung von Erneuerbare-Energien-Vorhaben, 2009, p. 246, and EnBW, Offshore Herausforderungen und Chancen, 2010, p. 3).

164 These expert opinions are usually based on the available data provided by the wind research platforms (FINO I-III), which have been installed in the North and the Baltic Sea near to the appointed OWP priority areas in the meantime. Such data further improves the quality and predictability of the wind conditions in the German EEZ and thus also of the potential cash flows to be generated by an OWP project. The FINO I-III data is freely available on the FMHA (*BSH*) webpage (see http://www.bsh.de/de/ Meeresdaten/Beobachtungen/MARNET-Messnetz/Stationen/fino.jsp (accessed 02 October 2011)) and should provide enough comfort to the banks when examining an OWP project, according to Mr. Dahlke. Furthermore, also valuable wind data from the Alpha Ventus test site becomes more and more available, where the measured wind conditions have exceeded the initial wind projections so far (see Appendix D, question 15).

165 Typical matters covered by such deductions are the electricity consumption of the OWP itself, expected inner park transmission losses and the OWP accessibility risk (i.e. weather risk). Normally, a deduction of 15 to 20% on the gross wind prognosis (*Bruttowindprognose*) or 10 to 15% on the expected wind farm efficiency (*Parkwirkungsgrad*) is considered by banks.

166 See Appendix E, question 1.

167 See Stiftung Offshore Windenergie, Wind vom Meer für saubere Energie/Offshore Wind for Clean Energy, undated, p. 5, http://www.offshore-stiftung.com/Offshore/ 128/109/94/60005/design1.html (accessed 03 October 2011).

go up to 90 to 100 m above sea level and are expected to rise even further in the future[168].

So, suitable technical concepts for the foundation (*Fundament*) and the remaining components of an OWG (tower, gondola and rotor blades) are necessary to withstand such a demanding environment and to keep any technical disturbances at a minimum.

An OWP project developer can choose between several established *foundation concepts*.[169] The foundation technique finally selected must fit to the specific conditions of the seabed at the respective OWP site and resist permanent large pressures. Foundation types typically used for German OWP are well established foundation concepts, which have been proven already in other offshore industries[170]. Hence, the selection of a suitable foundation concept is normally considered to be rather unproblematic by banks[171].

In contrast, technical experiences for the most sensitive component of an OWG, the *offshore wind turbine*, have been less comfortable for a long time because of a missing track record.[172] However, some progress was made in this regard lately, especially since the recent commissioning of the first OWP in Germany's EEZ. Today, wind turbines of up to a size of 5 MW are bankable when delivered by a well established supplier such as Siemens AG, REpower Systems SE or AREVA Wind GmbH[173]. In addition, remaining technological risks are further mitigated to a large extent by the availability/performance guarantees (*Verfügbarkeitsgarantien*) typically provided nowadays by the respective wind turbine supplier[174].

Hence, banks can rely on a much better track record in the meantime, but nevertheless still have an eye on the considerable technological risks related to an OWP project.

---

168 See Appendix D, question 14.

169 These concepts include gravity, monopile, tripile, tripod, jacket, bucket and floating foundation techniques (see KPMG, Offshore Windparks in Europa - Marktstudie 2010, 2010, pp. 42-43).

170 See Richter, Offshore-Windenergie in Deutschland: Potentiale, Anforderungen und Hürden der Projektfinanzierung von Offshore-Windparks in der deutschen Nord- und Ostsee, 2009, p. 60, http://www2.leuphana.de/umanagement/csm/content/nama/ downloads/download_publikationen/ 75-7_download.pdf (accessed 11 September 2011).

171 See Appendix E, question 5.

172 See Richter, Offshore-Windenergie in Deutschland: Potentiale, Anforderungen und Hürden der Projektfinanzierung von Offshore-Windparks in der deutschen Nord- und Ostsee, 2009, pp. 56 et seq., http://www2.leuphana.de/umanagement/csm/content/ nama/downloads/download_ publikationen/75-7_download.pdf (accessed 11 September 2011).

173 See Appendix E, question 5.

174 For further information see Section 5.1.6 below.

5.1.3 Installation

When it comes to the installation of an OWG, all necessary components of the OWG have to be transported to the respective OWP site in a first step. The transport itself usually does not cause any major troubles, whereas the second step, a proper installation of the OWG at sea, is a rather costly, risky and challenging mission, whose success is heavily depending on the applicable weather conditions[175].[176]

That is why banks, before entering into an OWP project, usually require that the necessary installation equipment has been reserved already by the project planner or the sponsors[177] and that the project's time schedule considers sufficient time buffer for potential construction delays due to unsuitable weather conditions.

Due to the enormous number of project contracts and interfaces the non-availability of a general contractor (*Generalunternehmer*) responsible for all steps related to the erection of an OWP used to be a major concern of many banks in the past (especially if the project was based on a project finance structure), but is now widely accepted.[178] Today, banks feel more and more comfortable with a so-called multi-contracting structure as many suppliers to the offshore wind industry nowadays offer much more integrated services and thus the number of project contracts has been considerably reduced (i.e. less contractual interfaces[179]). Moreover, positive precedents successfully using such contractual scheme are available in the meantime.

The positive developments mentioned above have led to a further reduction of uncertainty for banks, as well as to a better and more balanced allocation of the

---

175 Good weather conditions and a calm sea are essential requirements for the erection of an OWG (the suitable weather window often lasts only for about 120 days/year). Moreover, the older generation of installation vessels can be very often used only until waive heights of up to 1.5 m and wind force 5 (see Appendix D, question 11). However, new buildings such as the Jack-Up-Barge „Wind Lift I", used for the erection of the OWP "BARD Offshore 1" can be used in much harsher environments (waive heights of up to 5 m and wind force 7), which allows for more flexibility and an extended weather window (see BARD group webpage, http://www.bard-offshore.de/de/konzeption/errichtung/jack-up-barge (accessed 08 October 2011).

176 See Richter, Offshore-Windenergie in Deutschland: Potentiale, Anforderungen und Hürden der Projektfinanzierung von Offshore-Windparks in der deutschen Nord- und Ostsee, 2009, pp. 64 et seq.,http://www2.leuphana.de/umanagement/csm/content/ nama/downloads/download_publikationen/75-7_download.pdf (accessed 11 September 2011).

177 According to Mr. Dahlke sufficient offshore installation vessels should be available for the OWP scheduled to be erected in 2012/2013. In his opinion, the current lack of qualified personnel is the much greater challenge for the offshore wind industry (see Appendix D, question 11).

178 See Appendix E, question 6.

179 Nowadays, offshore wind turbine suppliers often also install and/or maintain the equipment delivered. Furthermore, project contracts normally consider a clear definition of the responsibilities of the respective contractual party (interface clause) (see Appendix E, question 6).

construction risks related to the installation of an OWP. Overall, this risk seems to be manageable nowadays for most banks seriously involved in the financing of OWP by the consideration of sufficient time buffers and cost reserves in the initial project planning.[180]

5.1.4 Insurance

When financing an OWP banks usually require an extensive insurance package to protect the project company by the transfer of part of the respective project risks to the insurers.

During the *construction phase* normally a Construction/Erection All Risks insurance (CEAR) is effected by the project company covering, inter alia, risks related to the transport of equipment, the construction and installation of the OWP, third-party liability, as well as insurance for (contingent) delay-in-start-up/advanced loss of profit. Contracted policies during the OWP' *operational phase* usually include standard insurances covering third-party liability, property and (contingent) business interruption risks (e.g. cable damages or defects[181]).[182]

The insurance market for the offshore wind industry used to be very tight in the past[183], but has made considerable progress in the last years. Tendered insurance packages for German OWP projects recently realised have been oversubscribed. Nevertheless, insurance is typically still only provided for the construction phase of the OWP and the first year of operation and must be renewed afterwards year by year. However, this procedure is not considered to be a significant risk by the banks

180 See Appendix E, question 6.

181 According to an analysis of the insurance broker MARSH, almost 75% of OWP' insurance claims observed so far are related to cable damage either within the cable network of the OWP itself or with respect to the sea cable connecting the OWP with the onshore grid (see Richter, Offshore-Windenergie in Deutschland: Potentiale, Anforderungen und Hürden der Projektfinanzierung von Offshore-Windparks in der deutschen Nord- und Ostsee, 2009, p. 71, http://www2.leuphana.de/umanagement/csm/content/nama/downloads/download_publikationen/75-7_download.pdf (accessed 11 September 2011).

182 See Appendix E, question 8 and Both, Die Rolle der Assekuranz bei der Entwicklung regenerativer Energieformen - am Beispiel der Windenergie in Deutschland, 2006, pp. 92 et seq., 153 et seq.

183 Only a few insurance brokers have been active in this field in the early days asking for high risk premiums, as these companies likewise had considerable problems for a long time to come to a precise assessment of the risks related to this industry.

anymore, as they can rely on a sufficiently deep insurance market for OWP today[184 185].

5.1.5 Grid connection

To be able to use the wind energy produced in an OWP out at the sea, the generated electricity must be transferred to the onshore distribution grids. The respective TSO concerned is required to establish such a grid connection by laying an undersea cable and cover all related costs caused[186]. At first glance, this looks straightforward. However, when going into the details one realises very fast that the establishment of an OWP' grid connection causes some uncertainties to all parties involved, including the banks which face an increased project risk in case of a delayed grid connection[187].

The typical main concerns of banks in this regard are the following:

a) Uncertainty about the point of time when the respective TSO has to start with the construction of the grid connection for a specific OWP and about any potential delays of the completion of that grid connection;

b) A lack of legal security in cases of a delayed grid connection suffered due to a force majeure event[188] and/or a disturbance of the grid once the OWP is operating; and

c) Limited available onshore grid capacity to properly process the electricity produced offshore.

In the meantime, project developers, banks and the TSO itself have much more transparency and planning reliability with regard to the first point, i.e. when the construction of the grid connection has to start, as the GFNA (*BNetzA*) position paper referred to in the previous section has defined very clear and objective grid connection criteria. Moreover, this paper also determines a maximum period until the

---

184 The standard insurance package typically contracted for conventional power plants is also available for OWP nowadays and can be provided by a much higher number of insurance brokers compared to some years ago.

185 See Appendix E, question 8.

186 See Sections 4.1.1.2 and 4.1.2 above for further information.

187 In these cases, banks would have to extend the life of the committed loans (*Kreditlaufzeit*) and continue to capitalise interest until the OWP finally starts to generate a positive operating cash flow once connected to the grid (see Appendix E, question 2).

188 In contrast, the risk of a delay due to TSO' negligent behaviour was already covered beforehand as the project company always had a claim for damages in such cases (see also Section 4.1.1.2).

respective TSO has to complete such a grid connection (30 months after the issuance of the TSO' conditional grid connection undertaking[189]).

In addition, the German legislator recently also tried to address the remaining problems outlined under b) and c) above in the course of the introduction of its supporting governmental measures (*Maßnahmenpaket*)[190]:

The extension of the payment of the feed-in tariff in cases of a delayed grid connection due to force majeure and/or subsequent disturbances of the grid improves the situation of the sponsors of an OWP and its financing banks, as the cash flow is no longer completely lost. However, one has to mention that such an extension only leads to a better restructuring case for the banks because of a longer tail.[191]

The German government has also streamlined the legal framework for the necessary extension of the onshore grids in Germany to allow for a proper processing of the electricity produced offshore and to reduce the need for curtailment of available total electricity production capacities in Germany in the future. However, German OWP and other renewable energy technologies are rather less affected by such a curtailment risk, as renewable energy can be fed into the grid with priority to conventional sources of energy[192]. Furthermore, even in the unlikely event that electricity produced by OWP in Germany has to be curtailed despite the aforementioned priority principle,

---

189 However, the TSO has to comply with such time limit only if it was not negatively affected by any circumstances out of its control. The existence of such provision is probably one of the main reasons why one can still observe delayed grid connections of OWP very often in practice. The TSO Tennet just announced to the German Ministry of Economics and the press that a punctual completion of grid connections is not possible due to a lack of capital, insufficient available capacities and delayed supplies (see Appendix E, question 2 and Handelsblatt, Tennet warnt vor Anschlussproblemen für Windparks, 2011, http://www.handelsblatt.com/politik/deutschland/tennet-warnt-vor-anschlussproblemen-fuer-windparks/5846652.html (accessed 27 November 2011)). The introduction of a clear definition by the German legislator what matters can be treated as a force majeure event out of the TSO' control and what matters not, would help to further reduce (legal) uncertainties of OWP project developers and the likelihood of a delayed grid connection. Delayed supplies to the TSO, for example, might be a matter which should be rather covered by sufficient liquidated damages to be agreed between the TSO and the respective supplier, which would at least reduce the financial risk of the OWP project company by the pass-through of such liquidated damages to it.

190 As of January 2012, the duration of the respective tariff payment (*Vergütungsdauer*) shall be extended in cases of delayed grid connection and/or disturbances of the subsequent electricity transmission even if the TSO has not acted negligently (see Section 4.3). Furthermore, the extension and optimization of the onshore distribution grids shall be accelerated by the introduction of the GEAA (*NABEG*) (see Section 3.2.3).

191 See Appendix E, question 3.

192 See Section 4.1.1.2 for more details.

the TSO would probably still be required to remunerate the respective OWP for the amount of electricity which could not be fed into the grid[193].

Overall, the introduction of the GFNA (*BNetzA*) position paper and the additional governmental measures outlined above, have clearly reduced uncertainties for OWP developers and banks with regard to the OWP' grid connection. However, even today a delayed connection of the OWP to the grid is still not unlikely in practice, which causes an increased project risk to the project parties. Thus, a punctual grid connection is still considered to be a major challenge for banks.

5.1.6 Operation & Maintenance (O&M)

A failure-free operation (*störungsfreier Betrieb*) of the OWP is very important, as every business disturbance or interruption reduces the amount of electricity produced and thus has a direct negative impact on the project company's operating cash flow (loss of revenue).[194] Furthermore, proper servicing and maintenance (*Wartung und Instandhaltung*) of an OWP is time-consuming, complicated and very expensive[195], as immediate access to offshore sites far out at sea is not always possible, due to prevailing weather conditions, especially in the winter season.[196] Hence, project developers try to maximize the technical availability (*technische Verfügbarkeit*) of OWG as much as possible, i.e. they try to reduce the need for costly maintenance measures to a minimum.[197]

193 However, it would be worthwhile to reduce remaining legal uncertainties in this regard by a further clarification through the legislator. Nevertheless, it is very unlikely that the German government would want the OWP project planners to bear the risk of insufficient available onshore grid capacity, as this would result in a materially negative effect on its plan to heavily extend available offshore wind energy capacities.

194 Please note that part of such risks can be usually mitigated by the use of certain structural elements (e.g. business interruption insurance or availability of supplier's performance guarantee). However, a complete "pass-through" of such risk from the project company to other project parties is usually not possible or would not make sense from an economical point of view (because this would come at too high costs).

195 "[...] O&M costs are the largest element of costs outside debt service" (see Robertson, Offshore Project Financing - Issues relating to wind farm developments in the UK, 2011, p. 58). Costs related to O&M account for about 25 to 30% of the total electricity production costs (see Bussel/Henderson, State of the Art and Technology Trends for Offshore Wind Energy: Operation and Maintenance Issues, undated, p. 1, http://www.offshorewindenergy.org/ca-owee/indexpages/downloads/Brussels01_ O&M.pdf (accessed 09 October 2011)).

196 Suitable weather conditions (weather window) are not only important during the OWP installation phase, but also and in particular when it comes to the maintenance of the OWP during its operating phase.

197 All components of an OWG are, for example, usually permanently monitored by a so-called condition monitoring system (CMS), which allows for an early detection of malfunctioning and/or erosion. Thus, operators are aware of technical problems very early, can react immediately, and further reduce down-times (see VDMA/BWE, The Wind Industry in Germany - Economic Report

In addition, offshore wind turbine suppliers nowadays typically also install and maintain the equipment delivered (full-service model) and provide availability/performance guarantees (*Verfügbarkeitsgarantien*), which considerably reduce the technological risks and uncertainties the project company and the financing banks are exposed to[198]. The establishment of such guarantees was a major step forward in achieving the bankability of an OWP project financing in Germany.

For financial institutions, a convincing O&M concept containing sufficient capacities of maintenance equipment and spare parts, qualified staff (located possibly even on-site), a condition monitoring system (CMS), and an adequate logistics supply chain (i.e. use of service boats and/or helicopters) is an essential element of a bankable OWP project. The quality of such concepts has considerably improved in the last years by the development of convincing O&M models, the availability of longer service agreements, the establishment of performance guarantees and more transparent and bankable contractual arrangements. Overall, the available O&M concepts are acceptable for banks today and the related risks are manageable.[199]

5.1.7 Overview of results

In the previous sections, the main bankability challenges related to a financing of an OWP in Germany have been discussed. Despite some (legal) improvement in the recent past, risks related to the OWP' grid connection, are still considered to be a major challenge by banks. In contrast, substantial progress has been made in the last years with regard to the risks of the offshore wind energy technology itself and the quality of available O&M concepts, which both are now classified rather as a medium

---

2009, 2009, p. 17, http://www.renewablesinsight.com/uploads/media/windindustrie_in_deutschland_en_02.pdf (accessed 09 October 2011)).

198 Availability/performance guarantees are usually provided by OWG suppliers for a minimum period of 5 years and consider a technical availability quota of 94% to 96%. However, in the meantime one can observe O&M agreements and performance guarantees in the market with even longer durations (e.g. up to 10 years or over the whole life of the banks' loans). OWP developers and banks should be aware that such guarantees typically specifically exclude the weather risk, which must be still borne by the project company (such accessibility risk is normally considered by banks through a deduction on the expected wind supply). The full-service model referred to above and offered by wind turbines suppliers strongly increases the likelihood to get finance for an OWP, whereas convincing O&M concepts provided by third parties are not yet available in the market (see Appendix E, question 5). For further details with regard to the main structural elements of this kind of performance guarantees refer to Busch, Ausgewählte vertragsrechtliche Fragen bei der Instandhaltung von Offshore-Windparks - Teil 2, 2011b, pp. 87 et seq.

199 See Appendix E, question 7.

challenge[200]. Furthermore, any insurance-related matters are no longer considered to be a significant risk affecting the bankability of an OWP project (for an overview of all identified main bankability challenges see Figure 8).

Compared to the situation two or three years ago, the banks' risks related to a financing of a German OWP could be considerably reduced by the implementation of supporting legal reforms by the legislator, practical and helpful solutions developed by the offshore wind industry (e.g. provision of wind turbine suppliers' performance guarantees, introduction of convincing O&M concepts) or the availability of a better (technological) track record in general.

OWP financing: main challenges and bankability issues:			
Subject matter	**Major**	**Medium**	**Minor**
Wind prognosis		X	
Technology		X	
Installation		X	
Insurance			X
Grid connection	X		
Operation & Maintenance		X	

Figure 8: Main bankability challenges

The remaining risks, which are to a large extent risks one would always be exposed to when financing an OWP project, are manageable by the banks by the consideration of adequate measures in the financing structure. It might be nevertheless helpful if policy makers, TSO and the offshore wind industry would mutually identify and implement further measures to overcome the current bottlenecks and uncertainties related to the OWP' grid connection. However, based on the above analysis, a well structured OWP project finance should be bankable in the meantime, even in today's challenging market environment.

200 Back in 2009, banks valued the technological risks related to the financing of an OWP and the available O&M concepts still as major challenges (see Richter, Offshore-Windenergie in Deutschland: Potentiale, Anforderungen und Hürden der Projektfinanzierung von Offshore-Windparks in der deutschen Nord- und Ostsee, 2009, p. 78, http://www2.leuphana.de/umanagement/csm/content/nama/downloads/ download_publikationen/75-7_download.pdf (accessed 11 September 2011)).

5.2 Financing OWP in Germany

Even when banks have concluded that the risks related to the described financing challenges influencing the financial viability of an OWP project are properly addressed, their ability to provide debt financing for such a project is dependent on two further aspects:

The individual project's bankabilty depends on the one hand also on the fact that the project is in line with applicable market practice (*banking standards*) and on the other hand that the general conditions influencing the bank industry's ability to lend must be supportive, which is vitally important when the substantial debt commitments needed for the financing of a capital intensive project like an OWP shall be secured in the banking market (*project placement*). Both aspects shall be briefly addressed in the following.

5.2.1 Typical banking standards in OWP financings

Typically, banks demand an equity contribution from the project sponsors in the amount of 30 to 40% of the total investment costs of the OWP, whereas 30% currently seems to be the absolute minimum. The maturity of the loan is determined on the basis of the rate and duration of the applicable feed-in tariff payment (*Vergütungshöhe und -dauer*) and usually corresponds to this period.[201] The minimum debt service coverage ratio (DSCR) of an OWP project, the main financial indicator for banks involved in project financings, should total at least 1.30 to 1.35.[202] Requested arranger fees usually amount to ca. 2% on the committed loan amounts, whereas debt margins for OWP projects typically lie in the range of 300 to 350 basis points above EURIBOR (allowing for an adequate risk/return profile for the financing banks)[203].[204]

---

201 Normally, committed loans are available during construction and a period of about 15 years after completion. However, the optional compression model recently introduced might allow for a higher project leverage, if acceptable for banks, and/or for shorter loan lives (e.g. construction phase plus 10 years after completion).

202 This ratio is based on the banks' base case (P90) and can partly depend on the quality of the respective supplier delivering the offshore wind turbines for the project.

203 See Merat, 288MW Meerwind IPP, 2011, p. 2, http://www1.ijonline.com/infrastructure financenews/preview?articleid=71999 (accessed 31 August 2011).

204 In contrast, the expected returns on equity for the sponsors/investors of OWP projects have been rather poor in the past (about 7%). Hence, mainly strategic investors, such as utilities and municipal energy suppliers (*kommunale Energieversorger*), have been active in this field for a long time, whereas financial investors have been rather reserved to invest. However, the increased initial feed-in tariff and the optional compression model recently introduced in the course of the additional measures (*Maßnahmenpaket*) passed by the German government, will lead to an improvement of the profitability of German OWP projects (returns on equity are expected to rise to about 12%; see KPMG, Offshore Windparks in Europa - Marktstudie 2010, 2010, p. 12).

Finally, banks request the establishment of typical structural elements of project financings, such as a debt service reserve account, an asset maintenance account and the implementation of a (project specific) cash sweep mechanism to further reduce the lenders' project risk.[205]

5.2.2 Project placement

Since the financial crisis in 2009, especially the financing of major projects like an OWP and its placement in the banking market has become much more complicated.[206] The total investment volume for an OWP in the German EEZ can easily amount to EUR 1.5 bn or more. The necessary debt financing normally requires a consortium of up to 20 banks.[207] However, only 10 to 14 banks have been regularly active in the field of OWP finance in the last years[208], which has led to a liquidity gap of about EUR 300 mn per project. However, such gap can now be remedied with KfW's special offshore wind energy state credit programme[209], which was considered to be "a major step towards ensuring the development of non-recourse financing in [Germany]" by the European Wind Energy Association (EWEA)[210].

Overall, the financing of an OWP to be built in the German EEZ used to be a considerable challenge in the past as only a few banks had the relevant expertise and were able to provide financing for such kind of projects. However, even in those days well-structured projects could get access to debt finance, whereas projects with a poor risk profile suffered difficulties or even delays securing a financing package. Today, more and more banks are interested to engage in the offshore wind segment in general.

---

205 See Appendix E, question 9.

206 Financial institutions all over Europe have reduced lending capacities and increased their risk sensitivity. Furthermore, lots of banks face problems to get access to funding in the interbank market, especially for longer maturities or foreign currencies. Currently there is no bank in the market willing to take the risk of an underwriting for a German OWP project (see Appendix E, question 11), which would provide much more planning security to the project planners. Hence, one can usually observe club deals in the market.

207 About 2/3 of the OWP' total investment costs of EUR 1.5 bn are usually provided by banks. However, banks are currently reluctant to commit a final take higher than EUR 50 mn per OWP project (see Appendix E, question 11), which requires available commitments of about 20 banks to realise the total debt funding needed for a project (in total about EUR 1 bn).

208 See KPMG, Offshore Windparks in Europa - Marktstudie 2010, 2010, p. 60.

209 See also Sections 3.2.2 and 3.2.3. So far, KfW has already provided substantial commitments to two OWP by using the new offshore wind energy state credit programme: KfW's committed loan amounts totalled to EUR 264 mn for „Meerwind" and EUR 280 mn for „Global Tech 1" respectively (see Börsenzeitung, Blackstone pumpt 700 Mill. Euro in Windparks, 2011a, and Börsenzeitung, KfW-Kredit für Offshore-Windpark, 2011b).

210 See EWEA, The European offshore wind industry - key trends and statistics: 1st half 2011, 2011b, p. 4, http://www.ewea.org/fileadmin/ewea_documents/documents/00_ POLICY_document/ Offshore_Statistics/20112707OffshoreStats.pdf (accessed 22 October 2011).

Additionally, the offshore wind energy credit programme introduced by the German government has further improved the situation. Hence, the ability to get funding for a well-structured and project finance based German OWP project and its placement in the banking market should no longer be an obstacle if complemented with the available governmental support schemes[211].

5.3 Security package

When setting up an (OWP) project finance, banks usually require an extensive security package. The question is: What is actually the function of such a security considering the fact that recovery rates of non-performing project financings are rather low?

The main objectives of providing security for a project finance are the defence of the project against third parties (e.g. unsecured creditors and suppliers), which might disturb the project by attaching a crucial asset or which might prevent a necessary restructuring of the project, and the control over its cash flow, or the project itself in case of a default situation (i.e. no business interruption because of the possibility to immediately step into the project with no court order necessary)[212]. Finally, banks have the right to realise and enforce security in case of an insolvency of the project company[213], which is usually considered to be the last step if all restructuring efforts have failed and all available alternatives to continue the project are less promising.

The typical security provided in the course of an OWP project financing is briefly described in the following *Section 5.3.1*, whereas the subsequent *Section 5.3.2* addresses some specialties with regard to the establishment of collateral over OWP/OWG located in the German EEZ.

---

211 Besides the use of KfW's special offshore wind energy state credit programme, other means of support are also available, such as loans to be provided by the European Investment Bank (EIB) or the provision of guarantees by export credit agencies such as Eksport Kredit Fonden (EKF), Denmark (see Appendix E, question 11).

212 See Wood, Project Finance, Securitisations, Subordinated Debt, 2007, p. 83 and White&Case, Rechtsgutachten zu der Anordnung von Sicherheitsleistungen für Offshore-Windenergieanlagen, p. 34, http://www.bsh.de/de/Meeresnutzung/Wirtschaft/ Windparks/Grundlagen/BSH_W%26C_Gutachten.pdf (accessed 15 October 2011).

213 See White&Case, Rechtsgutachten zu der Anordnung von Sicherheitsleistungen für Offshore-Windenergieanlagen, p. 34, http://www.bsh.de/de/Meeresnutzung/Wirtschaft/ Windparks/Grundlagen/BSH_W%26C_Gutachten.pdf (accessed 15 October 2011).

5.3.1 Usual elements of security in OWP project finance

In order to achieve the main objectives outlined above the banks' security package typically consists of the following elements (see Figure 9): a pledge over the project company's shares, a pledge over all project accounts[214], as well as an assignment of the project company's earnings, revenues, insurances and of all its rights under the project contracts (inter alia, the construction and supply contracts[215], the service and maintenance agreement, etc.[216]). In addition, all or at least the most important available assets of the project company[217] (i.e. especially all OWG being part of the OWP to be financed) will be transferred to the lending banks by way of security (*Sicherungsübereignung*).

Project finance security package	
- Pledge over SPC's shares; - Pledge over all project accounts; - Assignment of project's cash flows (e.g. earnings/revenues, insurances, etc.);	- Assignment of all rights under the project contracts; - Transfer of SPC's assets (*Sicherungsübereignung*); - (Direct agreements).

Figure 9: Typical project finance security package

The creation of such security is usually easy to implement with no legal uncertainties attached to it. However, when it comes to a transfer of assets within the German EEZ, where the vast majority of all German OWP is located, some peculiarities should be considered, which are outlined in the subsequent section.

5.3.2 Taking collateral in the German EEZ

The German legal system is not applicable per se in the German EEZ (no sovereignty[218]). This includes also the GCC (*BGB*), which does not contain an extension clause (*Erstreckungsklausel*) to the German EEZ. Therefore, the questions arises how a German law governed transfer of assets by way of security (*Sicherungsübereignung*)

---

214 Such as the SPC's earnings account, debt service reserve account or maintenance reserve account, etc. Thus, banks have access to all of the project's cash flows. Often, a so-called cash sweep mechanism is agreed on top, which requires the project company to prepay debt if sufficient funds are available.

215 Such as the supply contracts for the wind turbines, foundation and the transformer unit.

216 Although no real security claim is attached to this agreement, it shall be nevertheless mentioned at this point that banks normally also enter into direct agreements with all contractors to secure, inter alia, step-in rights for the project contracts (see Appendix E, question 10) which are inevitable to keep the project alive and running in case of a distressed scenario.

217 See Appendix E, question 10 and Wood, Project Finance, Securitisations, Subordinated Debt, 2007, pp. 84, 90.

218 See footnote 94.

can be properly effected in that area to avoid that the financing banks face any legal uncertainties with regard to their collateral.

Normally, such a transfer of assets is carried out at the place where the property is (finally) located. Despite the absence of an extension clause in the GCC (*BGB*), legal experts in Germany do agree that such legal statute should nevertheless also apply in the German EEZ[219], because German law has the closest legal connection (*engste rechtliche Bindung*) to such marine area. That is why a German law governed transfer of assets in the German EEZ should normally be valid and effective.[220]

However, to further reduce the banks' residual legal risk attached to taking collateral over the respective OWP supplies, alternative concepts have been developed and established in practice. All of them have in common that the transfer of ownership (*Eigentumsübertragung*) from supplier to buyer with regard to the assets serving as collateral to the banks will rather already take place when the GCC (*BGB*) is without doubt applicable. This could be, for example, at the base harbour, i.e. before the supplies are shipped to the respective offshore site or, alternatively, on a vessel flying the German flag[221].[222] By using such an approach, it is secured that the ownership of

---

219 See Lohse, Projektfinanzierung im Markt für erneuerbare Energien - Herausforderungen im Bereich Offshore Wind, 2009, p. 236.

220 When fixed to the seabed, the whole OWG would normally become an integrated part (*Bestandteil*) of the sea ground (*Meeresgrund*) of the German EEZ (see Article 94, 1 GCC (*BGB*)). When thinking about taking security, the problem is, however, that the German EEZ's seabed is actually no man's land and thus nobody can have land ownership (*Grundeigentum*) in it. Hence, a registration of a land charge (*Grundschuld*) covering also the OWG to be erected is not possible. To solve the problem, legal experts rather rely on Article 95, 1 GCC (*BGB*), which states that the OWG would not become an integrated part of the sea ground (*Scheinbestandteil*) if the fixing to it is only temporary (*vorübergehend*). This is usually the case, as the approval granted by the FMHA (*BSH*) requires that every OWG must be removed after 25 years (see Section 4.2.1.1). Hence, being rather considered as a movable (*sonderrechtsfähige Mobilie*), it is the common understanding of legal experts in Germany that OWG can be also properly transferred by way of security (*Sicherungsübereignung*) in the German EEZ. For further information see Wurmnest, Windige Geschäfte? Zur Bestellung von Sicherungsrechten an Offshore-Windkraftanlagen, 2008, particularly pp. 252, 259, 262, Diekamp, Sicherungsübereignung von Offshore-Windenergieanlagen, 2004, particularly pp. 19-20, 22, and White & Case, Rechtsgutachten zu der Anordnung von Sicherheitsleistungen für Offshore-Windenergieanlagen, p. 38, http://www.bsh.de/de/Meeresnutzung/Wirtschaft/ Windparks/Grundlagen/BSH_W%26C_ Gutachten.pdf (accessed 15 October 2011).

221 In practice the transfer usually takes place at the base harbour (Appendix E, question 10).

222 According to Article 929 GCC (*BGB*), it is necessary for the transfer of ownership of a movable that the supplier/owner delivers the asset to the buyer (*Übergabe*) and that both agree that ownership is to pass (*Einigung über den Eigentumsübergang*). The subsequent transport (*Verbringung*) of the assets to the offshore site in the German EEZ or the consideration of a condition precedent (*aufschiebende Bedingung*) according to Article 158 GCC (*BGB*) do not negatively affect the effectiveness of the transfer of ownership governed by German law, as it was constituted (*rechtsbegründet*) when the GCC (*BGB*) was clearly applicable (see also Müller-Helle/Theilmann, Eigentum und Eigentumsvorbehalt an Offshorewindkraftanlagen, 2010, pp. 371 et seq. and Ding-

the assets can be transferred legally effective to the buyer under German law. Thus, the subsequent buyer's transfer of assets to the banks by way of security is also not connected to any legal risks.

Despite the practicable solutions developed and introduced above to further reduce uncertainties of banks, the extension of the GCC (*BGB*) to the German EEZ would nevertheless be the best and most transparent option. By the implementation of this measure, the German legislator could arrange for much more clarity and additional legal certainty, as it would make it much easier to effectively take collateral over assets in the German EEZ.[223] However, the available practical solutions used so far are nevertheless working and should provide financial institutions sufficient comfort when financing an OWP in the German EEZ.

5.4 Chapter summary and outlook

The non-availability of sufficient debt financing for project finance structures used to be one of the major obstacles in the past when trying to realise an OWP project in Germany and the rest of Europe. It was almost impossible for long time to realise such kind of projects by the use of a project finance structure. Instead, loans have been rather granted on a corporate basis and mainly to strategic investors.

However, as outlined in the course of this section, the bankability challenges related to the financing of an OWP in Germany have been considerably reduced by the implementation of effective measures by the German legislator referred to in the previous sections, as well as by the offshore wind industry itself (i.e. provision of performance guarantees by wind turbine suppliers, better technological track record, improved O&M concepts, availability of satisfactory insurance packages, etc.). The remaining risks are manageable from the banks' point of view if the respective financial institutions are familiar with the offshore wind industry and have the relevant expertise to properly structure such kind of projects (e.g. by the consideration

er/Goldner, Sicherungsübereignung von Windenergieanlagen in der Ausschließlichen Wirtschaftszone, 2009, pp. 209 et seq.).

223 Since the OWG is treated as a movable (see footnote 220), one could alternatively also think of the possibility to register a mortgage for every OWG (along the lines of the registration of ship mortgages already possible at the FMHA (*BSH*)), which is not yet possible in Germany. Compared to the transfer by way of security (*Sicherungsübereignung*) normally used so far, such an alternative security concept might have the potential to provide even more legal certainty to banks. Being asked, Mr. Dahlke mentioned that a mortgage registration for OWG would be theoretically possible and the introduction of a respective register relatively easy to implement. However, he also noted that neither the offshore wind nor the financial industry have requested the introduction of such a security concept so far (see Appendix D, question 12).

of sufficient time buffers and cost reserves). Hence, nowadays the erection of an OWP in the German EEZ based on a project finance structure is bankable, if the project is in line with the applicable market standards of the banking industry and will be complemented with available governmental support schemes (e.g. state loans and/or guarantees), which is still essential to secure a successful project placement. The existing uncertainties of banks related to taking collateral over the assets of an OWP located in the German EEZ have been mainly mitigated by the practical solutions developed and described above. So, also in this regards banks should have sufficient comfort when financing an OWP.

Today, more and more banks are interested in the financing of (German) OWP, as the offshore wind industry is one of the very few fast growing industries where sufficient new potential for project financings at attractive rates is available. Furthermore, it is very likely that the investor base for OWP in Germany becomes more diversified in the future. Especially financial investors will probably tap the market more aggressively in the future by the use of non-recourse project finance structures and will be driven by the expectation to generate returns in the double-digit range. The increased allocation of capital by such investors is an important step to be able to reach the ambitious growth targets of the German government with regard to the available offshore wind energy capacities in Germany.

6. Summary

The purpose of this work was to analyse the general conditions in Germany for the realisation of OWP projects in the German EEZ. Particular focus was laid on the political environment, the applicable legal framework and the challenges related to securing a debt financing for this kind of major and technologically sophisticated projects (bankability).

Policy makers in Germany have supported the development of renewable energies already for more than two decades. This is even more so the case after the recent decision of the German government to completely phase out nuclear energy in Germany until 2022. The offshore wind energy sector plays a key role in the new German energy concept and shall contribute the major share of renewable energy to the future German energy mix. Hence, it is very unlikely that the positive sentiment of German politicians towards the offshore wind energy sector will change in the near future.

OWP project developers can also rely on a very stable and supporting legal framework in Germany. With regard to offshore wind energy, the legislator has, inter alia, established a fixed feed-in tariff, secured priority feed-in over conventional sources of energy, required TSO to connect OWP to the onshore grids and to cover the related costs, streamlined the OWP approval process, and defined wind energy priority areas in the German EEZ to facilitate the growth in this field. In addition, applicable conditions for the production of offshore wind energy will improve further once the additional governmental measures passed in 2011 become effective as of the beginning of 2012. Overall, the applicable legal environment in Germany nowadays should provide project developers sufficient incentives to invest as well as the investment security, legal certainty and planning reliability which are needed to realise an OWP project in the German EEZ.

Finally, securing a debt financing for an OWP to be erected in the German EEZ has been a major challenge for a long time, as the projects were exposed to considerable technological and other risks and the fact that the number of banks active in the offshore wind energy segment was often not sufficient to provide the amount of debt financing needed. In those days it was almost impossible to get funding for a non-recourse project finance structure. However, the offshore wind industry has made a lot of progress recently (i.e. especially provision of performance guarantees by wind turbine suppliers, better available technological track record and development of improved O&M concepts). The remaining risks are manageable by the banks in the financing structure. At the same time, the German legislator has successfully closed the funding gap referred to above by the introduction of its offshore wind energy state credit programme. Furthermore, more and more banks and financial investors intend to get active in the offshore wind energy industry based on the improved general conditions and the promising developments one could observe in this sector in the recent past. Hence, the realisation of an OWP in the German EEZ based on a project finance structure is bankable today, if the project considers applicable banking standards and is complemented by at least one of the available governmental support schemes.

Overall, prevailing conditions in Germany for the realisation of an OWP in the German EEZ constitute a very solid and reliable basis and should now be suitable to successfully support the targeted strong growth of the offshore wind energy sector in Germany. It is now up to the project developers and investors to make use of this opportunity and to let the German government's vision of a future German energy mix mainly based on renewable energies become reality. Let us hope for the best.

Bibliography

BMU (2007): EEG - Das Erneuerbare Energien Gesetz: Die Erfolgsgeschichte nachhaltiger Politik für den Standort Deutschland, Bundesministerium für Umwelt, Naturschutz und Reaktorsicherheit (BMU), 1st edition, Berlin.

BMU (2010): EU Commission approves state aid for offshore wind farm alpha ventus - Environment Minister Röttgen noted: Decision comes at the right time, press release No. 169/10, 30 October 2010, Berlin, http://www.bmu.de/ english/current_press_releases/pm/46658.php (accessed 29 October 2011).

BMU (2011a): Development of renewable energy sources in Germany 2010, Graphics and tables, Bundesministerium für Umwelt, Naturschutz und Reaktorsicherheit (BMU), Version: July 2011, Berlin, http://www.bmu.de/files/english/pdf/application/pdf/ee_in_ deutsch-land_graf_tab_en.pdf (accessed 22 October 2011).

BMU (2011b): Erneuerbare Energien in Zahlen - Nationale und internationale Entwicklung, Bundesministerium für Umwelt, Naturschutz und Reaktorsi-cherheit (BMU), 1st edition, July 2011, Berlin, http://www.bmu.de/files/pdfs/allgemein/application/pdf/ broschuere_ee_ zahlen_bf.pdf (accessed 22 October 2011).

BMWi (2011a): Der Weg zur Energie der Zukunft - sicher, bezahlbar und umwelt-freundlich, 06 June 2011, http://www.bmwi.de/BMWi/ Navigati-on/energie,did=405004.html (accessed 05 November 2011).

BMWi (2011b): Siebte Nationale Maritime Konferenz, Bundesministerium für Wirtschaft und Technologie, Dokumentation Nr. 597, 27. und 28. Mai 2011, Wilhelmshaven http://www.bmwi.de/BMWi/ Redaktion/PDF/Publikationen/ siebte-nationale-maritime-konferenz-2011-dokumentation,property=pdf,bereich=bmwi,sprache=de,rwb= true.pdf (acces-sed 02 October 2011).

BNetzA (2009): Positionspapier zur Netzanbindungsverpflichtung gemäß § 17 Abs. 2a EnWG, Bundesnetzagentur (BNetzA), http:// www.bundesnetzagentur.de/DE/Sachgebiete/ElektrizitaetGas/ Sondertheen/

AnbindungOffshoreWindparks/AnbindungOffshoreWindparks_node.html (accessed 09 September 2011).

Both, A. (2007): Die Rolle der Assekuranz bei der Entwicklung regenerativer Energieformen - am Beispiel der Windenergie in Deutschland, WiKu-Verlag, Duisburg & Köln.

Börsenzeitung (2011a): Blackstone pumpt 700 Mill. Euro in Windparks, issue 150, 06 August 2011.

Börsenzeitung (2011b): KfW-Kredit für Offshore-Windpark, issue 166, 30 August 2011.

Böttcher, J. (2009): Finanzierung von Erneuerbare-Energien-Vorhaben, Oldenbourg Verlag, München.

Britz, G. / Hellermann, J. / Hermes, G. (2010): EnWG - Energiewirtschafts-gesetz , Kommentar, C. H. Beck, München.

Bundesregierung (2002): Strategie der Bundesregierung zur Windenergienutzung auf See, January 2002, http://www.bmu.de/files/pdfs/allgemein/ application/pdf/windenergie_strategie_br_020100.pdf (accessed 30 October 2011).

Bundesregierung (2010): Energy Concept for an Environmentally Sound, Reliable, and Affordable Energy Supply, 28 September 2010, Federal Ministry of Economics and Technology (BMWi), Federal Ministry for the Environment, Nature, Conservation and Nuclear Safety (BMU), Berlin, http://www.bmwi.de/English/Redaktion/ Pdf/energyconcept,property=pdf,bereich=bmwi,sprache=en,rwb= true.pdf (accessed 30 October 2011).

Bundesregierung (2011): Entwurf - Erfahrungsbericht 2011 zum Erneuerbare-Energien-Gesetz (EEG-Erfahrungsbericht), 03 May 2011, http://www.bmu.de/files/pdfs/allgemein/application/pdf/eeg_ erfahrungsbericht_2011_entwurf.pdf (accessed 11 September 2011).

Bundesregierung (undated/a): 10 point immediate action program (*10-Punkte-Sofortprogramm*), http://www.bmu.de/files/pdfs/allgemein/ application/pdf/10-punkte-sofortprogramm_en_bf.pdf (accessed 30 October 2011).

Bundesregierung (undated/b): 10-Punkte-Sofortprogramm - Monitoring und Zwischenbericht der Bundesregierung, http://www.bundesregierung.de/nsc_true/Content/DE/StatischeSeiten/Breg/Energiekonzept/Sofortprogramm,property=publicationFile.pdf/Sofortprogramm (accessed 11 September 2011).

Bundesregierung (undated/c): Gesetz für den Vorrang Erneuerbarer Energien (Erneuerbare-Energien-Gesetz - EEG), Konsolidierte (unverbindliche) Fassung des Gesetzestextes in der ab 1. Januar 2012 geltenden Fassung, http://www.bmu.de/files/pdfs/allgemein/ application/pdf/eeg_2012_bf.pdf (accessed 11 September 2011).

Busch, R. (2011a): Ausgewählte (vertrags-)rechtliche Fragen bei der Errichtung von Offshore-Windparks - Teil 1, Neue Zeitschrift für Baurecht und Vergaberecht (NZBau), issue 1, 1 - 6, beck-online.

Busch, R. (2011b): Ausgewählte vertragsrechtliche Fragen bei der Instandhaltung von Offshore-Windparks - Teil 2, Neue Zeitschrift für Baurecht und Vergaberecht (NZBau), issue 2, 85 - 89, beck-online.

Bussel, G. / Henderson, A. (undated): State of the Art and Technology Trends for Offshore Wind Energy: Operation and Maintenance Issues, http://www.offshorewindenergy.org/ca-owee/indexpages/ downloads/Brussels01_O&M.pdf (accessed 09 October 2011).

BWE (2010): Positionspapier des Bundesverbandes WindEnergie e.V. (BWE e.V.) zur Novelle des Erneuerbare-Energien-Gesetzes, http://www.wind-energie.de/sites/default/files/download/publication/ bwe-positionspapier-zur-eeg-novelle-2012/bwe_position_eeg_ novelle_20110107.pdf (accessed 11 September 2011).

Dahlke, C. (undated): Verfahren nach SeeAnlV http://www.erneuerbare energien.de/files/pdfs/allgemein/application/pdf/dahlke_6.pdf (accessed 23 July 2011).

Dannecker, M. / Kerth, Y. (2009): Die rechtlichen Rahmenbedingungen für Offshore-Windenergieanlagen in der deutschen Ausschließlichen Wirtschaftszone (AWZ), Das Deutsche Verwaltungsblatt (DVBl), issue 12, 748 - 753.

Dena (2009): Offshore-Netze - Die Netzanbindung der Offshore-Windparks, Deutsche Energie-Agentur GmbH (Dena), Berlin http://www.dena.de/ themen/thema-esd/publikationen/publikation/ dena-factsheet-offshore-netze-die-netzanbindung-der-offshore-windparks/ (accessed 09 September 2011).

Diekamp, T. (2004): Sicherungsübereignung von Offshore-Windenergie-anlagen, Zeitschrift für Bankrecht und Bankwirtschaft (ZBB), issue 1, 10 - 22.

Dinger, F. / Goldner, T. (2009): Sicherungsübereignung von Windenergie-anlagen in der Ausschließlichen Wirtschaftszone, Zeitschrift für Bankrecht und Bankwirtschaft (ZBB), issue 3, 204 - 212.

EnBW (2010): Offshore Herausforderungen und Chancen, 1. Windenergieabend in Stuttgart, EnBW AG, 28 January 2010, http://www.wind-energy-network.de/downloads/EnBW__Hr._Dr.-Ing._Goetz__ Windenergieabend_ 280110.pdf (accessed 02 October 2011).

Ethik-Kommission (2011): Deutschlands Energiewende - Ein Gemeinschaftswerk für die Zukunft, 30 May 2011, Berlin http://www.bundesregierung.de/ Content/DE/__Anlagen/2011/05/2011-05-30-abschlussberichtethik-kommission,property=publication File.pdf (accessed 05 November 2011).

EWEA (2010): The European offshore wind industry - key trends and statistics 2009, The European Wind Energy Association (EWEA), http://www.ewea.org/fileadmin/emag/statistics/2009offshore/pdf/ offshore%20stats%2020092.pdf (accessed 22 October 2011).

EWEA (2011a): The European offshore wind industry - key trends and statistics 2010, The European Wind Energy Association (EWEA), http://www.ewea.org/index.php?id=1861 (accessed 22 October 2011).

EWEA (2011b): The European offshore wind industry - key trends and statistics: 1st half 2011, The European Wind Energy Association (EWEA), http://www.ewea.org/fileadmin/ewea_documents/ documents/00_POLICY_ document/Offshore_Statistics/20112707 OffshoreStats.pdf (accessed 22 October 2011).

Finkenzeller, K. (2011): Hart am Wind: Versicherer lassen sich Windparks teuer bezahlen, dpa press release: 14 June 2011, http://www.co2-handel.de/article343_16551.html (accessed 08 October 2011).

FMHA (*BSH*) (undated): Non-technical summary (North Sea): environmental report, http://www.bsh.de/en/Marine_uses/Spatial_ Planning_in_the_German_EEZ/ index.jsp (accessed 22 June 2011).

Frenz, W. / Müggenborg, H.-J. (2010): Erneuerbare-Energien-Gesetz Kommentar, Erich Schmidt Verlag, Berlin.

Gabler, A. (2010): EEG 2009 - Grundzüge der neuen Rechtslage für Anlagen- und Netzbetreiber: Netzanschluss, Einspeisung, Vergütung, Ausgleichsregelung, Rechtsschutz, EW Medien und Kongress GmbH, Frankfurt am Main.

Handelsblatt (2011): Tennet warnt vor Anschlussproblemen für Windparks, 16 November 2011, http://www.handelsblatt.com/politik/ deutschland/tennet-warnt-vor-anschlussproblemen-fuer-windparks/ 5846652.html (accessed 16 November 2011).

IEA (2010): World Energy Outlook 2010, International Energy Agency, 2010, France.

Kersting, M. O. (2011): Die Projektfinanzierung eines Offshore-Windparks, BKR - Zeitschrift für Bank- und Kapitalmarktrecht, issue 2, 57 - 63, C. H. Beck, München, Frankfurt am Main, Berlin.

KfW (2011): Merkblatt KfW-Programm Offshore-Windenergie, Kreditanstalt für Wiederaufbau (KfW), May 2011, http://k-f-w.net/kfw/de/I/II/ Download_Center/Foerderprogramme/ versteckter_Ordner_fuer_PDF/ 6000001940_M_273_Offshore_Windenergie.pdf (accessed 30 October 2011).

Klinski, S. (2001): Rechtliche Probleme der Zulassung von Windkraftanlagen in der ausschließlichen Wirtschaftszone (AWZ), Umweltbundesamt, Berlin.

Klinski, S. (2009): EEG-Vergütung: Vertrauensschutz bei künftigen Änderungen der Rechtslage?, Rechtsgutachten im Auftrag des Bundesministeriums für Umwelt, Naturschutz und Reaktorsicherheit (BMU), Berlin.

KPMG (2010): Offshore Windparks in Europa - Marktstudie 2010, www.offshore-stiftung.com/Offshore/61/61/60005/.../download.html (accessed 02 October 2011).

Lohse, O. (2009): Projektfinanzierung im Markt für erneuerbare Energien - Herausforderungen im Bereich Offshore Wind, Erneuerbare Energien (Band 1), Perspektiven und Strategien: Rechtliche und wirtschaftliche Aspekte, 221 - 238, K. J. Thomè-Kozmiensky, Neuwied (Beitrag zur Berliner Energiekonferenz 2009).

Maier, K. (2008): Die Ausdehnung des Raumordnungsgesetzes auf die Ausschließliche Wirtschaftszone (AWZ) dargestellt an der auslösenden Situation der raumordnerischen Steuerung von Offshore-Windenergieanlagen, Schriften zur Raumordnung und Landesplanung (SRL), Band 27, Selbstverlag Universität Augsburg / Technische Universität Kaiserslautern, Augsburg / Kaiserslautern 2008.

Mendonca, M. (2007): Feed-in Tariffs - Accelerating the Development of Renewable Energy, World Future Council, Earthscan, London.

Merat, A. (2011): 288MW Meerwind IPP, Infrastructure Journal, 24 August 2011, http://www1.ijonline.com/infrastructurefinancenews/preview? articleid= 71999 (accessed 31 August 2011).

Müller-Helle, A. / Theilmann, T. (2010): Eigentum und Eigentumsvorbehalt an Offshorewindkraftanlagen, Recht der Energiewirtschaft (RdE), issue 12, 2010, 369 - 375.

Nevitt, P. / Fabozzi, F. (2000): Project Financing, 7th edition, Euromoney Books, London.

Oschmann, V. / Sösemann, F. (2007): Erneuerbare Energien im deutschen und europäischen Recht - Ein Überblick, Zeitschrift für Umweltrecht (ZUR), issue 1, 1 - 8, Nomos, Baden-Baden / beck-online.

Richter, M. (2009): Offshore-Windenergie in Deutschland: Potentiale, Anforderungen und Hürden der Projektfinanzierung von Offshore-Windparks in der deutschen Nord- und Ostsee, Centre for Sustainability Management (CSM), Leuphana Universität Lüneburg, http://www2.leuphana.de/umanagement/csm/content/nama/downloads/download_publikationen/75-7_download.pdf (accessed 11 September 2011).

Robertson, N. (2001): Offshore Project Financing - Issues relating to wind farm developments in the UK, Refocus, Volume 2, Number 7, September 2001, 56 - 58.

Stiftung Offshore Windenergie et al. (2010): Positionspapier zur Offshore-Windenergie in Deutschland vom August 2010, http://www.eeg-aktuell.de/wp-content/uploads/2010/07/Positionspapier-zur-Offshore-Windenergie-in-Deutschland-August-2010.pdf (accessed 09 September 2011).

Stiftung Offshore Windenergie (undated): Wind vom Meer für saubere Energie / Offshore Wind for Clean Energy, http://www.offshore-stiftung.com/Offshore/128/109/94/60005/design1.html (accessed 03 October 2011).

VDMA / BWE (2009): The Wind Industry in Germany - Economic Report 2009, http://www.renewablesinsight.com/uploads/media/wind industrie_in_deutschland_en_02.pdf (accessed 09 October 2011).

Vinter, G. (1998): Project Finance, 2nd edition, Sweet & Maxwell, London.

Watson, Farley & Williams (2011): Erneuerbare Energien in Deutschland – Briefing, http://www.wfw.com/Publications/Publication891/$File/ WFW%20-%20Renewable%20Energy%20in%20Germany% 202011%20-%20GERMAN.pdf (accessed 11 September 2011).

White & Case (2011): Rechtsgutachten zu der Anordnung von Sicherheitsleistungen für Offshore-Windenergieanlagen, 08 February 2011, http://www.bsh.de/de/Meeresnutzung/Wirtschaft/ Windparks/Grundlagen/BSH_W%26C_Gutachten.pdf (accessed 15 October 2011).

Wood, P. (2007): Project Finance, Securitisations, Subordinated Debt, 2nd edition, Sweet & Maxwell Ltd., London.

Wurmnest, W. (2008): Windige Geschäfte? Zur Bestellung von Sicherungsrechten an Offshore-Windkraftanlagen, The Rabel Journal of Comparative and International Private Law, volume 72, 236 - 263, Mohr Siebeck, Tübingen 2008.

Wustlich, G. (2007): Das Recht der Windenergie im Wandel - Teil 2: Windenergie auf See, Zeitschrift für Umweltrecht (ZUR), issue 3, 122 - 129, Nomos, Baden-Baden.

Yescombe, E. R. (2002): Principles of Project Finance, Academic Press, San Diego/London.

Zeiler, M. / Dahlke, C. / Nolte, N. (2005): Offshore-Windparks in der ausschließlichen Wirtschaftszone von Nord- und Ostsee, promet, volume 31, no. 1, 71 - 76, Deutscher Wetterdienst 2005.

Appendix

A – Project finance definition

As mentioned already above, the possibility to raise debt for the erection of OWP in Germany via project finance structures will be crucial to comply with the defined governmental targets for the renewable energy production in Germany and the German offshore wind energy sector in particular. An OWP developer should therefore be familiar with project financing structures in general as well as the features which are typically attached to such financing schemes.

When reviewing the relevant literature, the following definition of the term project finance (*Projektfinanzierung*) is very often used: "*A financing of a particular economic unit in which a lender is satisfied to look initially to the cash flows and earnings of that economic unit as source of funds from which a loan will be repaid and to the assets of the economic unit as collateral for the loan*"[224].

At first glance, this definition might look a bit abstract, but this is very much the essence of how a project financing works. To get a clearer picture Appendix B additionally briefly summarizes the main characteristics which usually go along with such a financing scheme.

B – Project finance characteristics

The main characteristics of project financing structures to be dealt with in more detail below are typically a cash flow-based bank lending to a single purpose project company, a proper risk allocation between the individual parties involved in the project, non- or limited recourse vis-à-vis the project's sponsors, which usually want to keep such project off-balance and to go for a high leverage of the project (see Figure 10).

When implementing a project financing structure, usually a *single purpose company* (SPC) will be established, which has - as the name implies - only one purpose: the realisation of the specific (OWP) project itself. Naturally, a newly founded SPC cannot provide any backward looking track or business record for the banks to look at, when examining the project. That is why lenders solely verify whether the future

[224] See Nevitt/Fabozzi, Project Financing, 2000, p. 1. An alternative definition can be found in Lohse, Projektfinanzierung im Markt für erneuerbare Energien - Herausforderungen im Bereich Offshore Wind, 2009, p. 221.

expected cash flow of the project itself is sufficiently high enough and certain to repay the debt to be granted (*cash flow-based lending*).[225] Furthermore, sponsors usually do not hold a majority share of the project SPC to avoid the duty to put it on their balance sheet (*off-balance sheet structure*).[226]

Moreover, it is essential for the success of a project financing that the participants involved in the project can agree on an allocation of the respective risks attached to the project, which is finally acceptable for everybody (*suitable risk allocation*).[227] Those parties include sponsors and banks, but also suppliers, insurance companies and other parties involved. Usually, the basic principle of risk sharing in project financings is that the respective party which can handle and influence the specific risk the best, should also be responsible for it[228]. However, in reality the final risk sharing agreed is very often rather a question of negotiation power. Nevertheless, especially the banks involved must finally be satisfied with the risk sharing concept on the table, which is a main cornerstone to come to an overall bankable project financing structure.

In case of a pure project financing structure, the creditors of the project SPC usually do not have any recourse vis-à-vis the project's sponsors (*non-recourse*), i.e. the sponsors are only liable for their equity portion committed in the course of the initial project structuring, which means that - if the available cash should be short after the project has been implemented - neither of the sponsors is required to put additional funds into the project SPC. In practice, one can nevertheless observe that in some cases sponsors have provided at least some additional comfort to the SPC's creditors (e.g. provision of a payment or a completion guarantee, or a stand-by facility to cover potential cost overruns during construction). However, these measures are usually

---

225 Besides examining the future cash flow of the project/SPC, banks generally do require an extensive security package as per the Project Finance definition above. Please refer to section 5.3 for further information.

226 For further information see Lohse, Projektfinanzierung im Markt für erneuerbare Energien - Herausforderungen im Bereich Offshore Wind, 2009, pp. 223-224, Yescombe, Principles of Project Finance, 2002, pp. 7, 13, 15 and Böttcher, Finanzierung von Erneuerbare-Energien-Vorhaben, 2009, pp. 21 et seq.

227 For further information see Lohse, Projektfinanzierung im Markt für erneuerbare Energien - Herausforderungen im Bereich Offshore Wind, 2009, pp. 223-224, Yescombe, Principles of Project Finance, 2002, p. 16, and Vinter, Project Finance, 1998, pp. 24 et seq. (the latter source contains also additional information about possible risk allocation measures such as the "pass-through" of project risk and/or the possibility of "back-to-back" contracting).

228 See Lohse, Projektfinanzierung im Markt für erneuerbare Energien - Herausforderungen im Bereich Offshore Wind, 2009, p. 224 and Böttcher, Finanzierung von Erneuerbare-Energien-Vorhaben, 2009, p. 58.

limited to a certain maximum amount and/or a specific period of time (*limited recourse*).[229]

Finally, project financing structures are typically used to fund projects in very capital-intensive industries with relatively predictable future cash flows and thus typically come along with a relatively *high leverage* (70 to 90%).[230]

Project finance characteristics	
- Single purpose (project) company (SPC); - Cash flow-based lending; - Off-balance sheet structure;	- Suitable risk allocation; - Non- or limited recourse; - High leverage.

Figure 10: Project finance characteristics

The German offshore wind industry is no doubt a very capital-intensive industry. However, the precise prognosis of the generated future cash-flows is usually more complicated than in other industries due to the uncertainty about the future wind conditions at the respective OWP site. Hence, the leverage for OWP project financings in Germany's EEZ has, so far, been rather on the lower end of the above range if not even lower (i.e. rather 60 to 70%).[231]

C – Corporate structure description

The term "corporate structure" or "corporate loan" describes on-balance sheet lending to financially very solid companies (e.g. utilities). By setting up such a financing scheme, banks can rely on the strengths of the financial and economical performance of the respective corporate - usually a payment guarantee is provided by it - and thus do not necessarily have a look on the risks attached to the individual project to be financed (i.e. the offshore wind energy market and/or the OWP project's cash flow risk are of secondary importance). The funds needed for this kind of corporate

229 See Lohse, Projektfinanzierung im Markt für erneuerbare Energien - Herausforderungen im Bereich Offshore Wind, 2009, p. 223 and Yescombe, Principles of Project Finance, 2002, p. 7.

230 See Yescombe, Principles of Project Finance, 2002, pp. 5 et seq.

231 For a typical (OWP) project structure, the individual parties usually involved in this kind of project financing and a description of the specific phases an (OWP) project finance-based transaction will go through over its lifetime please refer to Lohse, Projektfinanzierung im Markt für erneuerbare Energien - Herausforderungen im Bereich Offshore Wind, 2009, pp. 225 et seq. and Böttcher, Finanzierung von Erneuerbare-Energien-Vorhaben, 2009, pp. 30 et seq.

structures can be usually collected very easily in the banking market (bankable structure).[232]

D – Transcript of FMHA (*BSH*) interview

The following transcript is of an interview with Mr. Christian Dahlke, Head of Division Management of the Sea (*Leiter des Referats Ordnung des Meeres*) at the FMHA (*BSH*), conducted on 23 September 2011 in Hamburg, Germany.

D. 1) FMHA (*BSH*) approval process:

Question 1:

Does the approval for the erection of an offshore wind park (OWP) in the German EEZ require a separate approval by the Federal Agency for Nature Conservation, FANC (*Bundesamt für Naturschutz, BfN*)?

Answer:
Yes. Such separate approval is necessary since the last revision of the Federal Nature Conservation Act (*Bundesnaturschutzgesetz*) passed in March 2010 (extension of law to the German EEZ). Additional separate approvals to be granted are the necessary approval for the connection of the OWP to the onshore grid as well as the approval by the respective Waterways and Shipping Directorate (*Wasser- und Schifffahrtsdirektion*).

However, with the recent revision of the Federal Maritime Responsibilities Act (*Seeaufgabengesetz*) and the amendment of the Marine Facilities Ordinance (*Seeanlagenverordnung*) currently in progress (probably to be passed end of 2011 or the beginning of 2012), the German legislator is seeking for a further streamlining of the OWP approval process, more legal certainty for OWP project developers, and finally also for a clarification of the competencies of the FMHA (*BSH*) itself. Upon the effectiveness of such legal changes, a separate approval to be granted by the FANC (*BfN*) is no longer necessary, which will significantly accelerate the OWP approval process. However, the FMHA (*BSH*) will nevertheless continue to consider statements and opinions of the FANC (*BfN*) when examining the application for the erection of an OWP.

---

232 For more details regarding the individual features of corporate structures on the one hand and project financings on the other see Böttcher, Finanzierung von Erneuerbare-Energien-Vorhaben, 2009, pp. 25 et seq.

Question 2:

The approval of the FMHA (*BSH*) for the erection of an OWP has to be announced to the public. Is it possible to object to such approval and, if so, who can do it and for how long is such objection possible?

Answer:

An objection (*Widerspruch*) can be submitted by everyone within one month after the respective approval has been announced, which has happened already in some cases in the past. After the expiry of this period the OWP investor is protected (*Vertrauensschutz*). However, if the FMHA (*BSH*) should gain new information subsequently which speak against the approval granted, it theoretically has the right to revoke it. However, such revocation (*Widerruf*) would probably result in the respective project developer's right to claim compensation for damages (*Schadensersatz*).

Question 3:

How often does it happen that the FMHA (*BSH*) receives competing applications for the same offshore site?

Answer:

It is not rare. The problem of parallel applications is real and a suboptimal constellation, which unfortunately cannot be avoided. A project developer can only rely on a kind of a gentlemen's agreement of the offshore wind industry that a second application for the same offshore site should not be submitted out of fairness vis-à-vis the first applicant.

Question 4:

Has the application for an OWP consisting of more than 80 wind turbines become possible in the meantime?

Answer:

Yes. However, in practice already the realisation of OWP with 80 or even 40 wind turbines has been a huge challenge so far. The larger the project, the higher is the amount of debt financing needed. Based on the experiences of the past, project developers should avoid to plan too big, as it is still not an easy task to secure a financing for an OWP. Furthermore, the higher the investment volume the more banks are needed to finance the project, and thus the efforts necessary to coordinate the banking consortium will increase accordingly and should not be underestimated. The split of a very large OWP project into smaller pieces, i.e. the application for several single approvals (e.g. 2 x 40 wind turbines) might be rather worthwhile, as the handling of the individual "sub-projects" is much easier (better marketing possibilities, lower overall investment volume, better ability of banks to diversify investments).

Question 5:

Does an approval granted by the FMHA (*BSH*) usually consider conditions for the commencement and the completion of an OWP?

Answer:
Approvals in the past considered a standard condition to start with the erection of the OWP within 2 years after the respective OWP has been approved by the FMHA (*BSH*). Such deadline could usually be extended if any occurred delays had not been the fault of the respective project developer. Today, conditions of that kind will be rather determined on a case-by-case basis, depending on the specifics of the individual project. A latest date when an OWP must be completed is normally not considered.

Question 6:

How long does a typical FMHA (*BSH*) approval process take in total and what is the average duration of the individual approval phases? The last available information is: first participation round (2 to 3 months); second participation round including application conference (8 to 9 months); conduction of environmental impact assessment, EIA (*Umweltverträglich-keitsprüfung, UVP*) (9 to 16 months); third participation round including discussion hearing (*Erörterungstermin*) and granting of final approval (8 to 10 months), i.e. 2 to 3 years in total.

Answer:
The first participation round is not mandatory and usually not conducted if the respective OWP shall be erected in a marine area where other OWP have been approved already, because authorities are already familiar with that offshore site and relevant information is also available to a certain extent. Also the duration of the conduction of the necessary EIA (*UVP*) is very much depending on whether the OWP shall be erected in a marine area on which considerable information is already

available or whether the respective area has not yet been examined. In the latter case, the EIA (*UVP*) phase will last at least 12 months or longer, whereas the period can be shorter if some information is already available. The indicated length of the last approval phase is clearly too long. If all requirements for an approval are met, its issuance is much more standardized in the meantime. A duration of 4 to 6 months is rather realistic.

Question 7:

Does the FMHA (*BSH*) always make use of its right to require security from the project developer to ensure an orderly removal (*Rückbau*) of the OWP facilities? What security is usually required/provided and to what extent? Is it possible to distinguish between the different project phases of an OWP (e.g. construction and operation phase)?

Answer:
If the FMHA (*BSH*) comes to the conclusion that security has to be provided by the project developer to ensure an orderly removal of the OWP facilities, it is obligated to require it. This is usually the case for every OWP project. Typically, a bank guarantee or a letter of comfort (*Patronatserklärung*) is provided, which can be replaced by a cash deposit after completion of the OWP or any other acceptable collateral. The security must be created upon the commencement of the OWP construction phase at the latest and must cover the complete expected removal costs throughout the whole project cycle (i.e. there is no discretion or risk-related differentiation possible). However, it is nevertheless possible to provide such security step-by-step for individual separable building phases. The expected removal costs are, inter alia, depending on the OWP project's distance to the coast as well as on its foundation technique used (e.g. the removal of a monopole is usually cheaper than any other alternative foundation type). Nevertheless, currently available knowledge about the potential development of OWP' removal costs is not sufficient. However, as a rule of thumb, one can state that the expected costs of removal might be slightly lower than the installation costs of the respective OWP.

Question 8:

The standard condition for maximum noise emission (*Lärmemissionen*) usually considered in the approval granted by the FMHA (*BSH*) leads to uncertainties for project developers and banks, because the compliance with that requirement is currently not possible by the use of any of the available technologies (especially during the construction phase of the OWP). How does the FMHA (*BSH*) deal with this matter in practice?

Answer:
The FMHA (*BSH*) is fully aware of this problem. On the other hand, it intends to keep the pressure on the industry to continuously invest in the development of suitable technologies enabling a further reduction of noise emissions which is as high as possible. However, when the erection of an OWP is nevertheless approved by the FMHA (*BSH*) and the respective project developer properly uses the agreed noise mitigation measures (*Lärmminderungsmassnahmen*), his position should be nevertheless protected (*Vertrauensschutz*), i.e. a stop of the construction is very unlikely as long as no better alternative technology is available. In addition, the Federal Environment Ministry (*Bundesumweltministerium*) is currently eagerly developing an offshore noise protection strategy (*Offshore-Schallschutzstrategie*) in order to increase the predictability of administrative action (*administratives Handeln*), to further reduce legal uncertainties and to provide for more planning security for the offshore wind industry. This strategy shall be passed still in year 2011.

D. 2) Federal Spatial Planning:

Question 9:

What status do the priority areas (*Vorranggebiete*) defined for the erection of OWP in the German EEZ have?

Answer:
By the introduction of the spatial planning the main source of conflict, namely the competition between different marine uses in certain marine areas, has been mitigated (*entschärft*). The identified offshore wind energy priority areas are clearly reserved for wind energy purposes, i.e. alternative marine uses are not allowed if in potential conflict with the possible construction of an OWP. Furthermore, these areas have the effect of a supporting expert opinion (*unterstützendes Sachverständigengutachten*) in the course of an OWP approval process, i.e. generally only project-specific matters or newly available general technical or environmental information can speak against an

OWP project (which was not available when the FMHA (*BSH*) defined such priority areas in the course of its spatial planning).

Question 10:

To what degree are the currently existing identified priority areas utilised by OWP projects operating, already approved or still in the process of being approved?

Answer:
The currently existing priority areas are fully planned (*beplant*). In the meantime applications have been submitted to the FMHA (*BSH*), which even consider the erection of OWP in marine areas outside the identified priority areas. According to the German legislator offshore wind energy shall have a capacity of 25,000 megawatt in 2030, whereas a full utilisation of the currently existing priority areas leads to an expected maximum capacity of about 10,000 to 15,000 megawatt. Hence, it is very likely that new priority areas in both the North Sea and even in the Baltic Sea (potential for approximately 300 additional OWG) will be determined in the course of 2012 to be able to further cope with the fast development of the industry and the German government's ambitious growth targets.

D. 3) Miscellaneous:

Question 11:

Does the offshore wind industry still face a shortage of installation vessels (*Errichter-schiffe*)?

Answer:
So far, only older and smaller installation vessels are available, which can be used for many purposes only until waive heights of up to 1.5 m and wind force 5. However lots of new ships have been ordered in the meantime, which are urgently necessary to cope with the requirements and growth of the industry. Once those vessels have been delivered sufficient capacity should be available. OWP starting with the construction phase in 2012 / 2013 should have nevertheless access to proper installation vessels, as the installation equipment is normally booked already in advance. The main bottle-neck of the offshore wind industry is rather a lack of qualified staff.

Question 12:

According to relevant German legal literature, an offshore wind generator (*Windenergieanlage*) in the German EEZ could be considered as movable (*sonderrechtsfähige Mobilie*), which would not become an integrated part of the sea ground (*Scheinbestandteil*) as the fixing to it is only temporary (*vorübergehend*) (see also Article 95, 1 German Civil Code (*BGB*)). Would it be possible to introduce a new register for offshore wind generators (OWG), where financing banks could for example register a mortgage as security (comparable with the FMHA (*BSH*) register of ships already in existence)?

Answer:
Yes, theoretically that would be possible. Actually, this is an interesting idea, which would not be too difficult to implement. We are currently setting up an overview of all OWG anyway (*Bauwerksregister*), which could be easily upgraded (*erweitert*) by the relevant features. I'm aware that some representatives of the offshore wind industry and the banking industry have cautiously indicated their interest in such possibility, but so far nobody has expressly requested the introduction of a register for OWG.

Question 13:

Did, in your opinion, the position paper (*Positionspapier zur Netzanbindungsverpflichtung gemäß § 17 Abs. 2a EnWG*) published by the German Federal Network Agency (*Bundesnetzagentur*) in October 2009 improve the planning reliability and investment security for OWP project developers?

Answer:
In my opinion, everybody involved in the process of the erection of an OWP has been able to see a bit clearer since the introduction of this position paper, including the project developers seeking for an approval from the FMHA (*BSH*).

Question 14:

What is the average size of OWG currently built in the German EEZ?

Answer:
One can observe hub heights (*Nabenhöhen*) of about 90 m and total heights of up to 150 m including the OWG' rotor blades (*Rotorblätter*).

Question 15:

A precise prognosis of the wind conditions at the marine site where an OWP shall be erected is essential not only for the project developer itself, but also for the banks providing financing for such kind of project. How do you evaluate the available data base in this regard (e.g. alpha ventus wind data, data provided by the FINO (wind) research platforms)?

Answer:
So far, wind conditions of the Alpha Ventus OWP where Repower and Areva OWG are tested have been better than expected. Especially the Repower OWG runs well. Furthermore, the (wind) data base of all three FINO research platforms is available for everybody on the FMHA (*BSH*) web page. Overall, the available information today should provide sufficient comfort for project planers, investors and banks.

Question 16:

What investor groups have mainly invested in OWP in the German EEZ so far?

Answer:
In the past, international utilities (*Energieversorger*) such as EnBW (Baltic 1 & 2 plus two new projects in the North Sea), RWE, E.ON (currently working on three OWP projects in the German EEZ) and Vattenfall (one German OWP project) have been very active. The only financial investor involved so far is Blackstone, who has already invested in one German OWP and is currently verifying possibilities to step into another project (inter alia, for economies of scale reasons). However, municipal utilities (*Stadtwerke*) too have been already active in the German offshore wind sector (e.g. Baltic 1, Borkum West II, Global Tech 1) and/or are very much interested in (further) investing into this field in the future.

Question 17:

How much offshore wind capacity is currently already operating in the German EEZ?

Answer:
In the Baltic Sea it should be about 48 megawatt (i.e. 21 OWG each with 2.3 megawatt) and about 135 megawatt in the North Sea (i.e. 27 OWG each with 5.0 megawatt).

Question 18:

Which foundation types are typically used?

Answer:

Monopile foundations are most common, but can only be used for OWG up to 3.6 megawatt located not too far out at sea. For 5- or even 6 to 7 megawatt OWG located in marine areas with higher water depths other foundations techniques have to be used (e.g. jackets, tripods). Gravity foundation techniques will be developed soon.

E – Transcript of KfW IPEX interview

The following transcript is of an interview with Mr. Mirko Sedlacek, Vice President in the renewable energies department of KfW IPEX Bank GmbH, conducted on 22 November 2011 in Frankfurt am Main, Germany.

E. 1) Financing challenges:

Question 1:

Adequate wind conditions at the marine area where an OWP shall be located are essential for the success of such kind of project. How do banks handle these issues in practice?

Answer:
Indeed, the available wind supply will always be one of the key risk drivers of an OWP financing having a direct impact on the project's revenues. However, such risk is manageable in the financing structure. Banks usually require wind yield assessments for the respective offshore site from two independent experts. Those opinions are normally based on the available wind data generated by the FINO research platforms. Today, such data becomes more reliable than a couple of years ago, as longer statistical series of wind data are available in the meantime and the first OWP already in operation start to produce valuable additional information in this regard as well. Furthermore, banks consider certain standard and project specific deductions on the forecasted wind supply based on the technical advice, for example for the OWP own electricity consumption, potential inner park transmission losses and the OWP accessibility risk (such weather risk must be usually borne by the project company). Deductions total to about 15 to 20% on the forecasted gross wind supply or about 10 to 15% on the expected wind farm efficiency (*Parkwirkungsgrad*), which normally already considers potential wake effects (*Abschattungseffekte*) occurring in the OWP.

Question 2:

A punctual connection of the OWP to the onshore grid used to be one of the major challenges for banks when financing an OWP. However, further progress has been made in this regard, for example by the issuance of the GFNA (*BNetzA*) position paper. How would you evaluate such grid connection risk today?

Answer:

The availability of the (unconditional) grid connection undertaking to be issued by the respective transmission system operator (TSO) is part of the conditions precedent package to be fulfilled before first drawdown. Moreover, the position paper of the GFNA (*BNetzA*) has added transparency by defining objective grid connection criteria, which when fulfilled result in a TSO' duty to issue such grid connection undertaking. As recently communicated by Tennet in a letter to the German Ministry of Economics and the press, the TSO sees significant challenges with regard to the construction of the offshore grid connection and the requirement of the 30 months construction period is expected to be exceeded in many cases. This is a situation which carefully needs to be analyzed for each individual project. A delay of the respective grid connection of an OWP would lead to a necessary extension of banks' loan lives and an increase of interest to be capitalised before the project's completion. Thus, the cash buffers normally considered in project financing structures (e.g. for potential cost overruns) could be eaten up or in the worst case could be even insufficient to cover the additional funds needed (normally a buffer for a delay of up to 6 months is considered in the project planning). Furthermore, the project might face additional costs due to the fact that reservations for necessary installation equipment must be extended. All in all, a delayed grid connection of an OWP still has a considerable impact on the project risk for sponsors and banks and is probably the current major challenge related to a realisation of an OWP in the German EEZ.

Question 3:

Are you of the opinion that such grid connection risk can be (partly) mitigated by the measures recently introduced by the German legislator (i.e. extension of payment period of feed-in tariff in cases of delayed grid connection - even in cases of force majeure - and/or subsequent disturbances of the grid)?

Answer:
This is a further step forward. However, mainly for project sponsors, as banks would still face longer loan lives and/or higher capitalised interests in such cases. Hence, such new legislation improves rather the restructuring scenario of banks (i.e. longer tails).

Question 4:

How do you evaluate the risk for curtailment for German OWP?

Answer:
Renewable energies, including offshore wind energy, enjoy priority feed-in in Germany. This is an essential element of Germany's renewable energy policy and considerably reduces such risk for OWP developers. Nevertheless, the fast and adequate extension of onshore grids is definitely one of the major tasks, which have to be tackled in the near future.

Question 5:

How do you assess the technology risk related to OWP projects in the German EEZ (what kind of wind turbines and foundation techniques are bankable in the meantime)?

Answer:
Wind turbines up to a size of 5 megawatt should be bankable nowadays if delivered by an established and reputable supplier such as Siemens, Repower or Areva. However, Siemens is still the leading supplier (best track record in the market as well as a financially very solid manufacturer). Compared to the situation about two years ago, one can rely on more valuable operating experiences today due to the commissioning of the Alpha Ventus test site and other OWP in Europe. Moreover, the technological risks project developers are exposed to have been reduced by the performance guarantees and warranties typically provided by the wind turbine suppliers nowadays, which become more standard in the meantime (wind turbine suppliers normally offer full service contracts including operation & maintenance (O&M)). Such guarantees usually cover an availability of ca. 94% to 96% excluding weather risk and are provided for periods between 5 and 10 years. Such concept is of course also very much appreciated by the banks, as wind turbine suppliers usually have the relevant expertise, valuable experiences (inter alia, gained from other OWP projects) as well as better access to the necessary equipment/spare parts. In return, alternative O&M concepts offered by independent third parties are not yet available in the market in broader terms for OWP. The foundation concept used for an OWP has no significant influence on the project's bankability as such. It is rather important

that the concept chosen is suitable for the respective project specifics. Overall, the technological risk is considered to be a medium challenge today.

Question 6:

How do you evaluate the risks related to the installation of an OWP (e.g. general contractor vs. multi-contracting, execution of interface agreement, availability of installation equipment)?

Answer:

It is very unlikely that a general contractor concept will become available in the offshore wind industry. However, the multi-contracting structures typically used have been refined further and are accepted by the banks in the meantime. Today, contractual parties usually enter into an Engineering, Procurement, Construction and Installation (EPCI) contract. By the use of such contractual arrangement uncertainties have been reduced compared to the contractual schemes used in the early days (i.e. less contractual interfaces). In addition, project contracts typically consider certain interface clauses which clearly define the tasks and responsibilities of the respective contractual party. Installation equipment, especially offshore installation vessels, should be sufficiently available today. Overall, installation risks related to an OWP are a medium challenge nowadays, which will be the case also in the future due to the missing general contractor concept. However, such installation risk is accepted by banks today and manageable by the consideration of adequate measures, cost reserves and time buffers in the project planning if experienced contractors are selected.

Question 7:

The availability of adequate operation & maintenance (O&M) concepts used to be one of the major challenges for the realisation of OWP in the past. How do you assess O&M risks and available O&M concepts today?

Answer:

O&M concepts are much more convincing today, as further progress could have been made by the offshore wind industry in this regard. The respective contractual arrangements now available are also much more accommodating. Moreover, wind turbine suppliers provide their performance guarantees for much longer periods in the meantime (up to 10 years or sometimes even for the whole loan life). Hence, available O&M concepts have improved compared to the situation some years ago. Today, banks consider the O&M risks related to the realisation of an OWP rather to be only a medium challenge compared to the situation 3 or 4 years ago.

Question 8:

What insurances are typically effected for an OWP project and how would you evaluate today's possibilities to insure such kind of project?

Answer:
During the construction phase of an OWP usually a Construction/Erection All Risks (CEAR) insurance (*Allgefahrenversicherung*) is effected to cover all risks related to its erection, such as transport risks, construction/installation risks, third party liability and (contingent) delay-in-start-up risks (i.e. loss of revenue due to a delayed project completion), whereas typical insurances to be effected during the operational phase of an OWP are (contingent) business interruption, third party liability and so forth. Today's available insurance packages for OWP are more or less in line with those available for the financing of every standard conventional power plant. The insurance market normally provides coverage for the OWP construction phase plus the first year of operation. Afterwards, the relevant insurance package must be renewed every year. Overall, insurance related matters are handled well on recent deals from a banks' perspective (no significant risk) as today's insurance market for OWP is much more developed and insurance packages for new OWP projects are normally even oversubscribed. We hope the underwriting volume available, remains adequate with a larger number of projects to be financed.

E. 2) Financing OWP:

Question 9:

What are typical banking standards when financing an OWP in the German EEZ (e.g. minimum capital, financing tenors, DSCR, etc.)?

Answer:
Sponsors usually would have to provide a capital contribution in the amount of 30% to 40% of total investment costs. The compression model recently introduced allows for shorter financing tenors (i.e. faster repayment of bank loans and lower refinancing costs for banks) and higher sponsors' returns, but also for a potentially higher leverage. However, a capital contribution of 30% is the absolute minimum observed in the market to date. Moreover, also KfW's new offshore wind energy credit

programme considers a minimum capital contribution of one third. Maturities of loans to be granted depend on the duration of the feed-in tariff payment for the individual project. Normally, banks do not want to be exposed to any market risk. Hence, the committed debt should be completely repaid during such period. In the past, banks have usually financed the construction period plus up to 15 years after completion. In case one chooses the optional compression model mentioned before, loan lives after completion could possibly come down to around 10 years. Debt service coverage ratios (DSCR) typically lie in the 1.30 - 1.35 range based on the lenders' base case (P90) and also depending to a certain extend on the quality and track record of the respective wind turbine supplier. Other standards normally considered are typical project finance elements, such as a debt service reserve account, an asset maintenance reserve account and a (project specific) cash sweep mechanism.

Question 10:

What types of security do typically belong to a bank's collateral package if (project) financing an OWP and when does the transfer of assets to the banks usually take place (legal uncertainties in the German EEZ)? Are direct agreements also typically part of the project structuring?

Answer:
An OWP security package normally consists of a pledge over the project company's shares and all project accounts, an assignment of all earnings, revenue streams and insurance claims, an assignment of all rights under the project contracts and finally a transfer of all assets. Furthermore, financing banks enter into direct agreements with all relevant project parties (e.g. agreement of step-in rights). The timing of the transfer of assets depends on the individual project structure. However, if possible, assets will be often transferred already in the harbour before being shipped to the respective OWP site in the German EEZ to avoid any legal uncertainties with regard to the effectiveness of such security.

Question 11:

What are in your opinion the essential elements for a successful placement of a German OWP in the banking market?

Answer:

The performance guarantees, which are provided by wind turbine suppliers nowadays, have been a major step towards the overall bankability of such technologically sophisticated projects. Furthermore, it is in our view still necessary to use at least one of the available governmental support features to secure a debt financing for a German OWP, such as guarantees provided by Danish EKF (if possible) or direct loans granted by the EIB or KfW under the existing credit support programmes. Especially, the introduction of KfW's offshore wind credit programme this year has considerably improved the possibility to secure a debt financing for the next 10 OWP to be erected in Germany in the future (closure of liquidity gap). Other helpful elements for a successful project placement are of course the use of well established suppliers (especially with regard to the wind turbines), the availability of a convincing O&M concept, the optional compression model recently introduced by the legislator and last but not least the expertise the respective project sponsors contribute to the project.

However, today more banks are interested to get active in the field of offshore wind energy in general compared to the situation 2 to 3 years ago. More than 20 banks have participated in European OWP projects in the meantime. The maximum ticket size per bank amounts to ca. EUR 50 mn. In addition, more and more banks want to tap the offshore wind sector with a more structured approach and thus develop respective offshore wind strategies (i.e. determination of preferred suppliers, max. commitment, etc.). Some of the banks' interest might be also based on the fact that the offshore wind sector is currently one of the very few fast growing industries where a sufficient number of large project financings for adequate risk/return profiles becomes available in the banking market (the lack of projects in other typical industries suitable to set up project financings leads to a highly competitive environment and thus often to very poor conditions for banks). Nevertheless, there is currently no bank in the market which feels in the position to provide an underwriting for an OWP project. However, this is a general observation in today's market environment and not specifically related to the offshore wind industry.

Question 12:

Corporate structures have been mainly used in Europe for the financing of OWP in the early days of such industry. Which German OWP project was the first one successfully placed in the banking market by using a real project finance structure (non- or limited recourse)? When did the closing of such transaction take place?

Answer:

Indeed, it was difficult to set up project finance structures for OWP projects in the past. However, with Borkum West II, Global Tech 1 and Meerwind, three German OWP project financings have been successfully placed in the banking market in the meantime. The first one was Borkum West II, which was closed in December 2010. All three of them have been real non-recourse project financings. So, OWP projects in Germany can be successfully financed by the use of a non-recourse project finance structure in the meantime if such transactions are well structured.

Question 13:

Do the OWP projects to be financed in the German EEZ come along with an acceptable risk/return profile for banks?

Answer:

The conditions for banks one can currently observe in the market are adequate given the risk profile of the projects. So far, the profitability of German OWP was rather a problem for the project sponsors themselves, especially if financial investors have been involved in the project structuring. However, the optional compression model now available should make an investment into such kind of projects also for those investor groups more attractive compared to projects in the UK for example.

<u>E. 3) Miscellaneous</u>:

Question 14:

Do banks face any uncertainties with regard to the mandatory approval to be granted by the FMHA (*BSH*), which is necessary for the erection of an OWP in the German EEZ? Is such approval a condition precedent, which has to be fulfilled before the first drawdown?

Answer:

The availability of such approval is definitely one of the necessary conditions precedents which have to be fulfilled before the money can be drawn under the available facilities, i.e. it will be in place before banks have to fund for the project. Subsequent to the issuance of its initial approval, the FMHA (*BSH*) must issue three independent construction permits (*Baufreigaben*), the first one after having examined the overall project in general, the second after the assessment of the detailed project design and the final third permit for the commencement of the OWP construction. Usually, not every of the aforementioned permits is available before banks would have to start funding at least part of their loans, i.e. theoretically there is a marginal risk that the FMHA (*BSH*) could ask for certain adjustments of the project design after first disbursement, which could cause additional costs and financing needs to the project. Those issues need to be managed in the financing structure.

Question 15:

Are there any other issues/problems with regard to the realisation of OWP in the German EEZ?

Answer:
One problem which gets more and more into the focus due to the strong growth of the offshore wind sector are the limited capacities of the (sub-) suppliers to such industry. A punctual supply of the components initially ordered might become a challenge if larger numbers of OWP are realized in parallel.

F – Map German EEZ Baltic Sea[233]

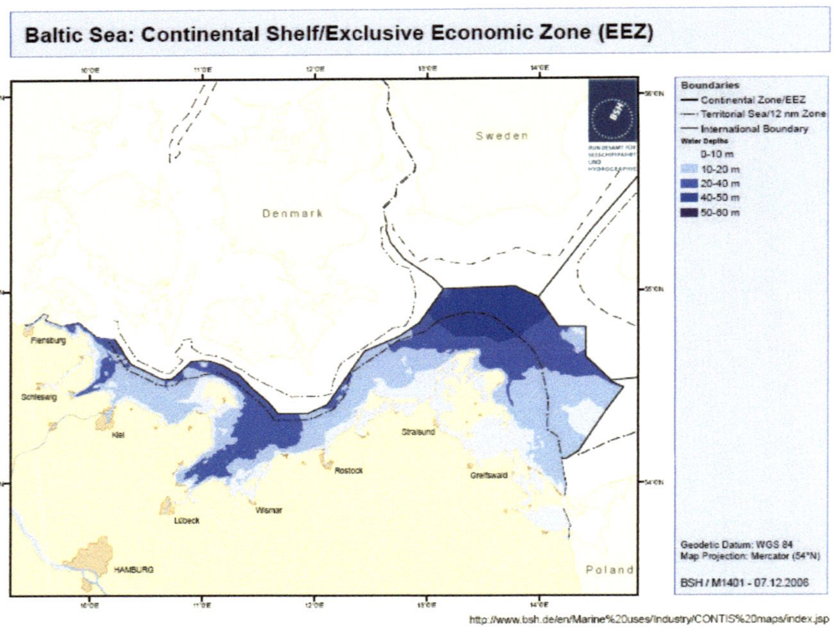

233 See FMHA (*BSH*) web page, http://www.bsh.de/en/Marine_uses/Industry/CONTIS_maps/BalticSeaGermanContinentalShelfExclusiveEconomicZone.pdf (accessed 12 November 2011).

G – Map German EEZ North Sea[234]

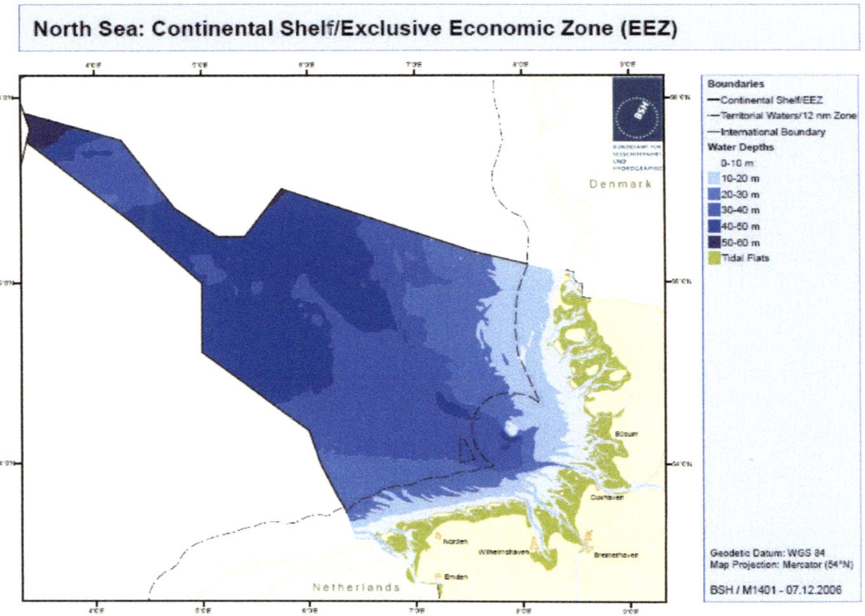

http://www.bsh.de/en/Marine%20uses/Industry/CONTIS%20maps/index.jsp

---

[234] See FMHA (*BSH*) web page, http://www.bsh.de/en/Marine_uses/Industry/CONTIS_maps/NorthSeaGermanContinentalShelfExclusiveEconomicZone.pdf (accessed 12 November 2011).

H – Map OWP Baltic Sea[235]

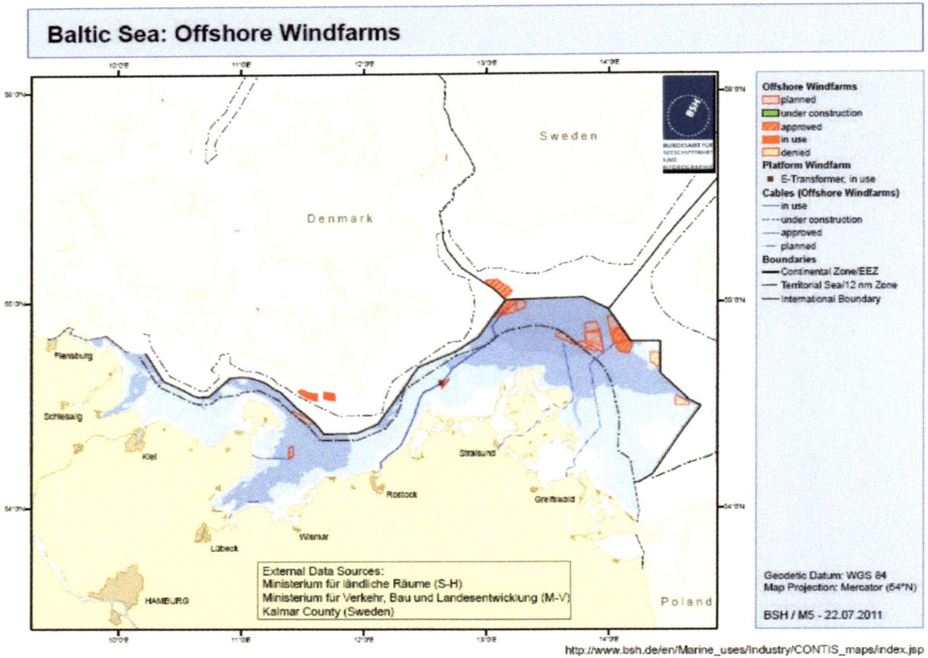

235 See FMHA (*BSH*) web page, http://www.bsh.de/en/Marine_uses/Industry/CONTIS_maps/BalticSeaOffshoreWindfarms.pdf (accessed 12 November 2011).

I – Map OWP North Sea[236]

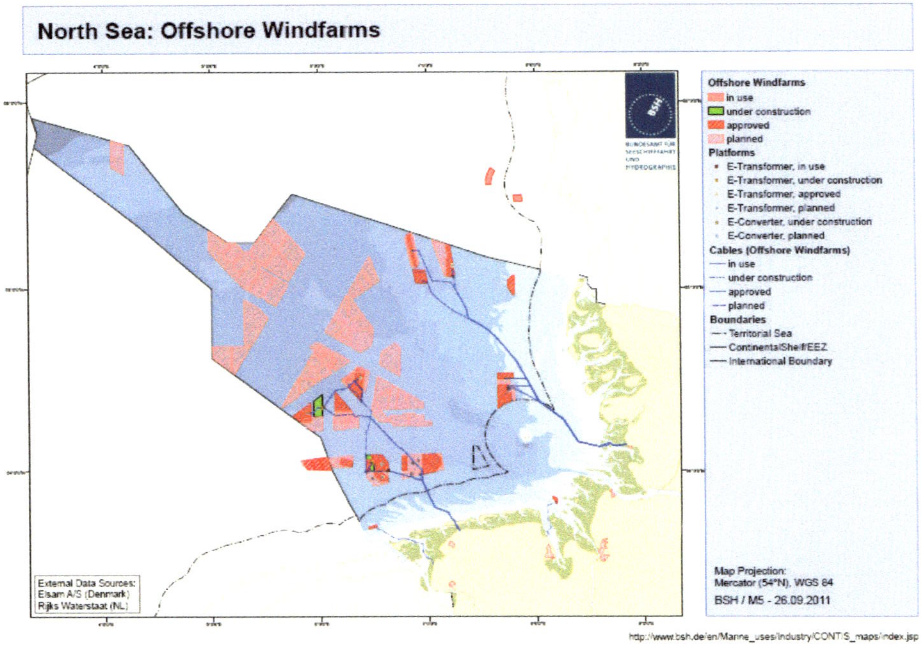

236 See FMHA (*BSH*) web page, http://www.bsh.de/en/Marine_uses/Industry/CONTIS_maps/NorthSeaOffshoreWindfarmsPilotProjects.pdf (accessed 12 November 2011).

J – Map Spatial Planning Baltic Sea[237]

Spatial Plan for the German Exclusive Economic Zone of the Baltic Sea - Map -

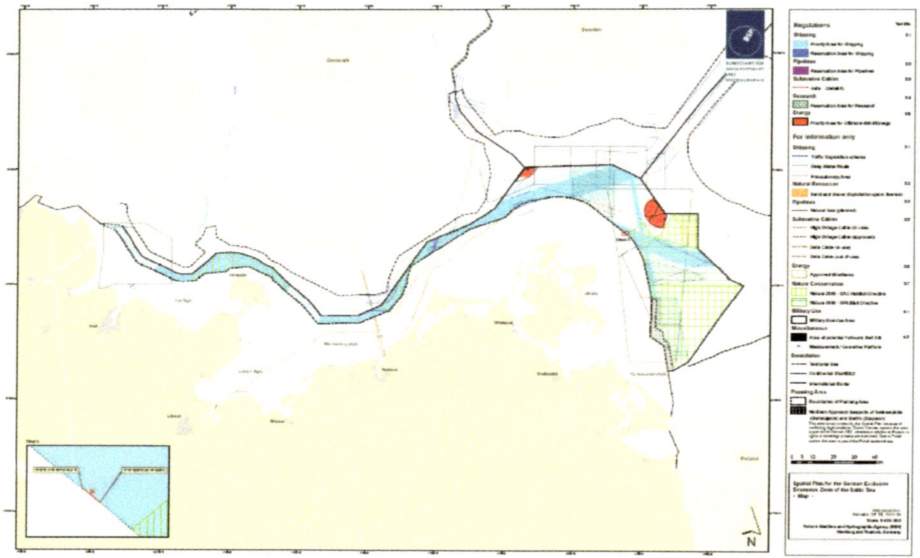

[237] See FMHA (*BSH*) web page, http://www.bsh.de/en/Marine_uses/Spatial_Planning_in_the_German_EEZ/documents2/MSP_DE_BalticSea_Dec2009.pdf (accessed 12 November 2011).

K – Map Spatial Planning North Sea[238]

Spatial Plan for the German Exclusive Economic Zone of the North Sea - Map -

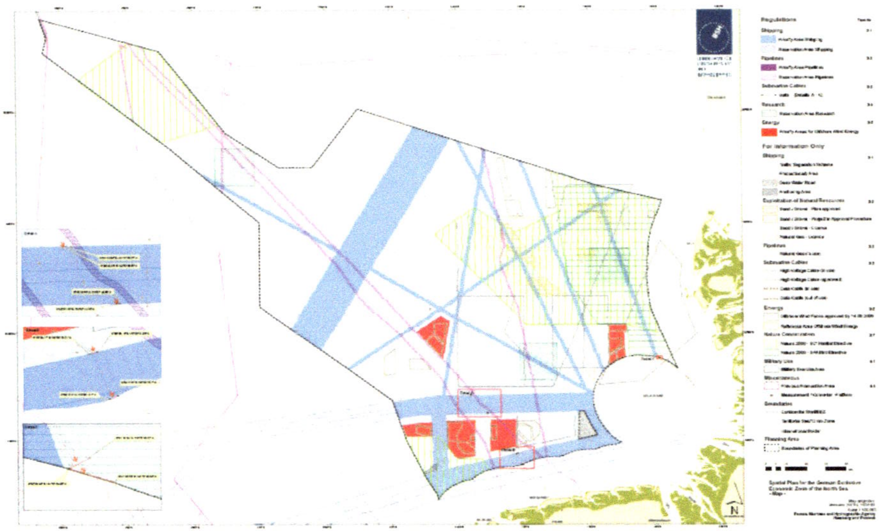

[238] See FMHA (*BSH*) web page, http://www.bsh.de/en/Marine_uses/Spatial_Planning_in_the_German_EEZ/documents2/MSP_DE_NorthSea.pdf (accessed 12 November 2011).